DOING THE HOMEWORK

Class Notes From the School of Life

Lawrence Jacklin

BALBOA.PRESS

A DIVISION OF HAY HOUSE

Cover design by Lawrence Jacklin
Author photo by Deirdre Jacklin

Balboa Press books may be ordered through booksellers or by contacting:

Balboa Press
A Division of Hay House
1663 Liberty Drive
Bloomington, IN 47403
www.balboapress.com
844-682-1282

Because of the dynamic nature of the Internet, any web addresses or links contained in this book may have changed since publication and may no longer be valid. The views expressed in this work are solely those of the author and do not necessarily reflect the views of the publisher, and the publisher hereby disclaims any responsibility for them.

The author of this book does not dispense medical advice or prescribe the use of any technique as a form of treatment for physical, emotional, or medical problems without the advice of a physician, either directly or indirectly. The intent of the author is only to offer information of a general nature to help you in your quest for emotional and spiritual well-being. In the event you use any of the information in this book for yourself, which is your constitutional right, the author and the publisher assume no responsibility for your actions.

ISBN: 978-1-5043-5258-1 (sc)
ISBN: 978-1-5043-5259-8 (e)

Library of Congress Control Number: 2016911975

Print information available on the last page.

Balboa Press rev. date: 04/24/2024

Dedicated to my sister, Marilyn, whose early birthday gift gave birth to this book.

And to my wonderful wife, Deirdre, for lovingly allowing me and this process to evolve, and to become.

TABLE OF CONTENTS

Preface

This book started as all books do – as a collection of empty pages. In this case, literally as a "blank book" given to me by my sister as an early birthday gift. The intent of that gift was to consolidate many years of poetry into *"one-place"*.

A poem is somewhat like a photograph of One Instant, One Event, One Perspective. The focus may be adjusted from the microscopic to the infinite, back again; and everywhere in between. And while I collected those scattered poems for sorting and review, I quickly realized two things: first was the fact that there were far too many to be contained in that small gift book; the second thing was a growing awareness that all of the poems which resonated the most with me now were following a theme, and these favored poems were also inspiring me to write new, related pieces. And write I did!

These new poems poured forth in the proverbial flood of thoughts and emotions; and then it hit me…I was writing a book! It was the story of my spiritual quest to understand God and the Universe. And although there are also poems about the intellectual side of these truths and their basis in scientific fact, there are far more about the emotional impact of learning these truths. This Emotional Journey is the story I want to share.

And I want to share the viewpoint of a person who has learned, at least in part, some of the answers, as well as the perspective of someone who is *still learning* these *Facts of Life*. The truth, of course, is that we will *All*, always *Be* learning these lessons, always gaining a deeper, fuller understanding of each answer; for this is the way of Life.

And although this book is not intended to teach, or be any form of workbook, we all learn from each other, and it is my hope that if I phrase something "just so" or use a particular word, I may help others to better understand these Truths at some level deeper than the mere intellectual grasp of a concept.

These poems are the pictures of my journey to Now.

Like many artists, I've always felt that my very best work has always just "come to me" without any great conscious effort. This is most certainly the case for the great majority of the poems here. As if, for a very brief moment, I became the *"Voice of the Universe"*.

But I am only one voice among Many who speak the Words of the Universe, and I can only offer one more perspective to help in understanding these ancient Truths.

Introduction

When I was about twelve years old, I was "Damned-to-Hell-Forever" by our parish priest – for having chosen to sleep in one Saturday and thereby miss a catechism class. The first thing that entered my mind after the Panic and Fear started to subside was that this damnation could not be from the God I was learning about in catechism. The second thing was the question: "Then, *What Is God?*"

That was my last day of catechism; and the first day of my Great Spiritual Quest.

I started going to church with friends – Baptists, Protestants, Methodists, etc. – to get their perspective on God and sin. But I repeatedly encountered something that seemed to be shared by all of these sects – Catholics included. That was the claim of each sect that *They* were Saved, and everyone else was Damned. Little babies were Damned! Yet there was Always a "Loving God"…It just didn't make any sense to me.

So I started studying those "other" religions – Islam, Hindu, and Buddhism – and they All had some good points, but still not *The Answers* which I sought. So I looked into various philosophies – Confucianism to Nietzsche's Übermench; and, as my father was a member of the Free Masons, I also explored several systems of magic – from Wicca to the Golden Dawn. And again, they All had their good points, but… eventually I kinda put together "My Own Religion" and left it at that for several years.

Then one day while I was working a booth at our county fair, on break I started talking to a woman who was also on break. She was working at the *Baha'i* booth. What? Here was "My Own Religion" right down the line:

There is only One God.
There is no Heaven and no Hell.
All Religions teach the Same Spiritual Truths.
All of these Teachers are Equal.
Men and Women are Equal.
All of the Races are Equal.
The Individual Investigation of Truth is a Sacred Obligation. (New to me, but I really liked it!)
And this one – straight from the pen of Baha'u'llah:
Science and Religion *must agree* – If they Do Not, *Then follow Science.*   (Wow!)

This last one was amazing to me! I had seriously considered several careers in the sciences, and science still holds a fascination for me now, although I tend to see it in a different light than I did then…

It was only a few days later that I became a Baha'i. And even though they profess to recognize All Other Religions as also being "Right", there was still an underlying sense of: *"We're Righter!"* So a few years later it was back to "My Own Religion", but by this time I was pretty much saying that I was *Spiritual*, but *not* religious.

I also took the *Silva Mind Control* course (taught by a Jesuit priest!), read the *Don Juan* books, and the *Seth* books, got an introduction to *Ramtha*, and *Mafu*, and a few other non-corporeal beings, and of course I encountered many New-Agers. And some of them were pretty amazing people, but I just felt most comfortable with "my own", and *Quantum Physics* was looking better every day…

I believe now, that even at the age of twelve, some part of me knew that questions asked with Passion and True Longing will Always be Answered. Much later I learned that the Answers will always be at a level that matches your Ability to Understand. Still later I learned that the best answers – the Truest and the Clearest Answers have No Words at all. They are Pure Emotion: Awe and Wonder, Astonishment and Joy.

But words are tools to aid communication – painting pictures which may be shared with others. And for many basic concepts, words are the simplest way to convey the essence of a particular idea.

Words give the Mind something to hold on to, until the Heart has found the Feeling of it.

———————————————

Author's Note:

It is Not my Intent – It is Not my Desire – to *Change* Anyone's Mind. It is Only My Hope that I might be able to Help *Open* just One Mind.

Poetry As Art:

One of my earliest Poet-Hero's was *e.e. cummings.* And one of my favorites was the Word "grasshopper" jumping all over the page. I too have "Grasshoppers", but I'm All About UPPERCASE! And punctuations and Such. But *cummings* is my primary inspiration for the presentation of My Written Word. But that Presentation becomes a visual experience as well – because of My GraSsHopPers. Because of my spacing and placement of words, sometimes even Letters themselves. Or the Direction a word or a phrase may travel across the page.

The result is somewhat akin to an Abstract Pencil Drawing. And the Images may be read like Clouds on a lazy autumn afternoon. Sometimes Dancing Figures. Sometimes Seahorses. Sometimes Tantric Mandela's. Sometimes DNA molecules. Sometimes GraSsHopPers.

And as a Poet, I have ulterior motives. First is the Fact that the Human Eye-Brain does Not Naturally flow across the page from left to right; it Jumps all Over – Down, Up, Sideways, and Through! And being Confronted by this Forced Confusion FORCES the Brain to Think a Little Differently – sorta LooSeNs-uP the Neurons…This is Scientific Fact.

The Second Ulterior Motive is Simple. It Sl o w s you Down and Makes you Pay a little More attention tO the WrittEn WoRd. Kinda makes you ThinK about iT more!

So Pay Attention!

———————————

Chapter One

In the Beginning

"A thought, even a possibility, can shatter and transform us"
Nietzsche

Preludes

<u>WE</u>

We are Star-Stuff
We are Burning Gases

We are the Earth
And
the Ashes

The Universe Spinning
Circling about Us

Ours to Choose
to
Win or Lose –

No Greater Freedom could be Known
than
The Future Is Our Own!

———————

Deirdre and I were talking one night about God and Life and Stuff, and she asked me if I had ever Thanked the priest who had "Damned me to Hell" and set me on my Life-Path. I said, no. She said I really needed to do that. Hence the following:

<u>Confession</u>

Bless me, Father, for I have Sinned.

But it was not as you, Spokesman of God, had proclaimed. You damned a twelve-year-old boy to Eternal Hell – for telling the Truth. For actually having made an adult-like choice. For exercising Free Will. And in that instant I KNEW you were WRONG! And I damned *You* in my mind. *That* was *my* Sin – to strike back Thoughtlessly, as a Child might.

I did not understand enough at Twelve to know that I should have Thanked You. I should have thanked you for Setting me Free. I should have thanked you for setting me on my Life-Path: my Great Quest to find God – to discover the Truth.

Of course at Twelve I didn't even know that *That* was what had occurred. I only knew that your Damnation was Wrong and that somehow that made what you had taught me about God wrong too. And all those thoughts were almost unconscious – almost like an Instinct. But I remember *The Question* that screamed in my mind:

"If He is Wrong, then What Is God?"

And the lesser questions washed over me – *What am I? What is Life?*

Why are we Here? Is there really a God, a Heaven, a Hell?

I was hurt and confused and kinda scared – and feeling very small and alone. But I was also very determined to get my answers even if it took a Lifetime!

So I thank you, Father, with all my Heart. I hope you will forgive my Sin against you. I did not understand then that your Wrong *against* me was Right *for* me.

Bless You, Father…

A few days later I wrote this:

is
Not Honored with Sunday Services
And Guilt-Laden Sermons which destroy Self-Worth

My God! We're "Born in Original Sin" –
What the Hell is *That* about?
You can't even decide whether to Pee or Cry –
And you're *Already* Damned?

And isn't it Amazing
that Original Sin
is
Knowing!

GOD is Not Honored with Lists –
Dos and Don'ts
Awaiting Rewards and Punishments

GOD Does Not Judge!

A Parent cannot Love one child More than another child
All are Equal
Unique but Equal

And If there is No Judgment
There can be No Punishment – No Hell

And there need Be no priests or ministers Telling Others
How They Must Live

No –
GOD is Not Honored
with Ritual and Fear

GOD is Honored in the Joy of Living
In the Dance of Freedom

GOD is Honored
When His Children Accept His Gifts
With Laughter and Joy of Heart
And Give Thanks with Song
And Love

*In Singing and Dancing
Is the Voice of the Law*

Hakuin

Part one – leaving the church

<u>Disillusionment</u>

"The Bible"
I remember always thinking
the *Name* itself
Was something *Magical*
Mysterious
Powerful

Then in high school I found out
it means "Book"
That's it – just "book"

Wow! Shattered Delusions…

Makes you wonder though –
They didn't even call it
"the Book of God"
?

———————————

<u>The Old "Father" God</u>

Long White Hair
A Full Head of Hair –
(Who would Believe in a Bald God?)

Long White Beard
Not so Fashionable Now –
But Still Impressive!

And those Glorious White Robes!
Who's His Tailor
?

Old man figure implies Once-young man figure –

Did He have a Letter-Sweater in high school?
And who changed His diapers?

It just doesn't Work for me –

Never Did
Never Will

———————————

Those Old Time Religions

Ya gotta love the Old Time Religions
(or not)
Every one of them tell you that God cannot be Defined
Then they all pretty much give you The Same Definition:

Omnipotent   Omniscient   Omnipresent
Infinite   and   Eternal

And truly, these Words which Describe God
Are Not your run of the mill Conversationally Common Words
And the *Definitions* of those words
Fall to the Outer Reaches of Reason and True Understanding:
Omnipotent – All Powerful
Like Ten Billion-Billion Atomic Bombs
are NOTHING

Omnipresent – Everywhere: At Once!

Omniscient – This one seems
Almost Straight Forward
But This is a Two-Sided Coin
And very few ever even Think to examine the Other Face –
It's the Face the churches don't talk about

Eternal – Never having had a Beginning
Never to have an Ending
There Is No Comparison
We live in a Dimension of Change
A Dimension of Time
There is Nothing
Nothing, Nothing, Nothing
Like It
Nothing Close

No – God is not an easy concept to Understand
Only the most Abstract Thoughts come Close
God Is truly Beyond our ability to Understand

But Not Beyond our Ability to Experience!

But instead of promoting the Wonder of this Limitless Being
Instead of Leading us
To The Overwhelming Serenity of this Experience
The churches try to sell us
Picture Post Cards of God
Wise Old Man on Throne
Stalwart Warrior in Gleaming Armor

Ya gotta love the Old Time Religions
(or not)

"I cannot believe in a God who wants to be praised all the time."
Nietzsche

<u>Yes, Virginia</u>

Yes, Virginia, there really Is a God.
But the Real God is Not the god of the churches –

Remember, Virginia, the god of the churches
Punishes
– Sometimes for Ever and Ever –
And the god of the churches only Rewards
people who Do as they are Told!

The god of the churches does not even allow people
to *Think* what they want –
Even if it's just a Question like yours…

But the god of the churches
Is only like a Story made-up by Bad Parents
Who try to make their children behave in a Certain Way
By Scaring Them

The Real God is Never Scary, Virginia
And *Never Ever* Punishes Anyone
The Real God only and always *Loves*
All of His Creations

And remember too, Virginia, that the Real God isn't a Man or a Woman
The Real God is Much Too Big to be like a Person
That's just an easy way to *talk* about God

The Real God is Wondrous and Mysterious beyond our imagining!

And through all of Time there have been many Teachers
Who have tried to tell us about the Real God
To just *Remind* us, really –
because deep inside ourselves
We already know about the Real God

We can look about the world and See
The Dance of God –
Everywhere
Ever Constant
and
Ever New

This is the Real God, Virginia
Growing before our Eyes!

And even though the Real God will not *Do* anything For us –
There is no Need
For He has Already given us the Greatest of All Gifts –
He made – *Each of Us* – His True Children
He made *Each of Us* to Be like *little* Gods
To Imagine like God
And to Create like God –
For we Each have
All the Power of God deep within ourselves
And we are Each Free to Be
Whatever our Hearts tell us to Be

You see, Virginia, when God made us,
He made our Hearts extra special –
Our own Heart is where *Each of Us* can Talk to God
About Anything!
And we never have to be afraid of God

And deep in the center of our Hearts, God will tell Each who Asks
What Special Gifts – what Talents – He has given to *That* person
To Give to the World –
That is really Why *Each of Us* is Here
To give a Gift that only *We* can give

We, *Each of Us*, have a very special place in the World
And the Real God will guide us to *our* place, each step of the way
If we will learn to *Listen* to the Voice of our Heart –
Our Heart can take us Anywhere!

And That is Why we should never try to be Anything
That does not make our Heart Joyful –
Regardless *Who* tells us to be That Way

And always remember, Virginia, that the Real God is Not
Just for Christians or Just for Hindus
or Just for Muslims
or Just for Jews
the Real God is within Each and Every One of us

The Real God is within You, Virginia
and Me, and Everyone
And the Real God is within all the Plants
And all the Animals
And the Rocks and within the Earth itself

The real God is within the most distant Star –
And always
As close as your very own Heart
Yes, Virginia, there really *Is* a God.

———————————————

<u>Untitled</u>

There are still days I wish
God, the Father, would reach down
Pat my head and say, "It's alright, My Son"

maybe Hug me

<u>Why I Say GOD</u>

Why do I so often use the word
"GOD"
?

There are any number of Other Words, Phrases –
And, forgive me if I offend
But in my opinion
"GOD"
Is probably the single ***Worst*** word!

Which God?!   Whose God?!
You must say, Allah!
You must not say, Yahweh!
God is on Our Side!
Nah, Nah!   Blah, Blah…

There is So Much Confusion and Conflict
Over this one Word

"the Universe" is better –
"the Universal Subconscious Mind"
"the Ground of Being"
"All That Is"
"The Source"
"That Which Is"
"The All"
And my Personal Favorite – The Seneca Indian:
"Great Mystery"
That one Nails it for Me!

So – Why *Do* I use "GOD" so frequently?
I'm a lazy S.O.B. –
It takes Less Time
Less Space
Less Effort

Cope!
It's just a *Word…*

A Conversation Between Strangers Passing on a Sidewalk

First Person: *"Oh, My God!"*

Second Person: *"Don't be Greedy."*

Wishful Thinking

I recently heard a wise man say:
"God is Too Big for any One Country."

And I So Wished he could have Gone-On:
*"God is Too Big for any One Planet
Or any One Solar System."*

*"The Universe is so Big
Because That's How Big
God is."*

*"There is no Throne
Big Enough to HOLD God."*
*"The Universe is God's Body,
and God's Soul is Bigger than That."*

*"We are Made
In the Image and Likeness of Our Creator."*
"We are Boundless"
"We are Limitless"

WE ARE!

It's wishful thinking –
But it really *IS* time
To get "The Message"
Out-There
AGAIN...

Part two – science and religion agree

<u>Tag – You're It!</u>

There is an Energy in the Universe
But "Energy" can be rather vague
– even a little Technical –

It's a Single-Thing
– inseparable –
So some call it a Field…
also kinda vague
And sorta Two-Dimensional sounding

And it's not Really *in* the Universe
That puts it some Place
But it's *in* Every Place
And *in* Every Non-Place

Some call it Pure Potentiality
Others call it Intention, or Spirit, or God…
But it Doesn't Matter What you *call* IT
No Word
No Ten Billion Words
Can even come Close to describing
IT

You can Experience IT
But you can never Explain IT
IT is not just *in* Every Thing –
IT *is* Every Thing

IT *Is* Us
And We *Are* IT

TAG!
You're IT!

———————

Quantum Physics To the Rescue!

I guess it's the little bit of the scientist that's always been
Part of who I Am –
But I've always felt that
"What Is God?"
Should have a Logical Answer
Not Physical Proof – Just Something that *Made Sense*

Quantum Physics Makes Sense
Not the Math and Formulas, Etc. – to *Me* –
But the Concepts, the Ideas behind the Numbers
They Make Sense

They Point to the Idea – the Realization – that God
Is not some Thing, some Where
But that God *IS*
EveryWhere, EveryThing, EveryWhen
Here and *Now*

That the Universe Itself is All One
One Immeasurable "Field" of Pure Energy
One Unimaginable Intelligence
Everything Connected to Everything Else
Sub-Atomic Particles Communicating
Faster than the Speed of Light!

The Realization that Matter as we Think of It – Does Not Exist

The things we *Perceive* as *Things*
Are All *Energy*
Gathered in Like Frequency to *Appear-As*
Chairs
Rocks
Trees
People
Air
Water
Every Thing

And this Energy is always in Motion
Little "Pieces" of this Energy Jumping
From one Form to Another
One instant part of a Person
The next – part of a Table
Now part of a Distant Star!
Yet Always
All is One

The Realization that Any One Particle Effects the Whole
And the Whole Responds to the One
And We Are Part of the Whole
And the Energy of the Whole Responds to Us

All the Universe
Every Dimension
Is
All
One

One Field of Energy
One Field of Consciousness
And it is All *Evolving* Right Now
Right Here

There is No Beginning
There is No End
It All Just *IS*
And
We Are Part of the Whole
Part of This
Great Oneness

We are Humans – Being
Evolving

————————

Profound Universal Truth #193

If Ever You cease to Grow
Cease to Evolve
On That Day
You will surely Be
As Dead As Dead Can Be

————————————

The Lessons of Quantum Physics

Two-Thousand Years Ago – and Before –
These Lessons were Taught
And Quantum Physics is now starting to Verify
These Teachings of the Mystics and the Avatars –
The Universe Is One Unified-Field of Energy

God Is Omnipresent

Matter and Energy Are the *Same Single Thing*
Expressing Itself in Different Forms –
And this Matter-Energy possesses *Consciousness*
Pretending to be Separate Things

All Is One – All the Dimensions
All the Multi-Verses are Connected
This Energy is *Conscious* and Communicates with Itself
Everywhere!
God Is Omniscient

This Matter-Energy is All One-Energy
The Form does not change the Essence of this Energy
God Is Everywhere – Turn over a Rock and There Is the Father
Turn it over in your hand – You are Holding God!
All Is God

This One-Energy is the Basis of All Form
And Is *Influenced*
By *Our* Thoughts and Emotions
As Ye Believe – So Shall It Be Done Onto Thee.
As Ye Sow – So Shall Ye Reap!

Thou art Made in the Image and Likeness of God

This Matter-Energy
Has Always Been and will Always Be
Before Abraham Was, I Am!
God Is Eternal

This Matter-Energy
Has No Boundaries
No Limits
God Is Infinite

Matter and Energy are One
They are Interchangeable
And can neither be Created nor Destroyed
Thou Art Eternal

We are Part of this One-Energy
Part of this Whole
The Immensity of Our *Self* is beyond all Imagining
Beyond all Comprehension –
On and On We Stretch
Into All the Dimensions of Space and Time
The So-Called "Parts" of our Self
Intertwining For Ever and Ever
We Are Infinite
We Are God

This Matter-Energy is Evolving
Ever Changing
Not in *What* It Is
Only in *How* It Is
And It molds ItSelf
To the Expectations of Each
There are Many Rooms in My Father's Mansion
God Is Omnipotent

We Each Create the World We See
Our Thoughts and Emotions
Send out Electro-Magnetic Energies into the Universe
And Like Energies are Returned to Us
As Things
Experience
Emotion

Always and in All Ways –
We Are the Creators
We Are God!

———————

<u>ReThinking the World</u>

We need to Change
The Way we Think!
The way we Think about God
The way we Think about the Earth
The way we Think about Life
The way we Think about Ourselves
Even
The way we Think about
Thinking

We need a ***New Language*** –
Scientists say that when we learn
a New Language
It not only Changes the Way we Think
But it actually Changes our
Brain –
The Physical Structure of that Organ
Creating new Connections
New Pathways
Allowing Old Pathways
Old Ways
To Fade Away

The following words will be included in our next Vocabulary Test:

Attraction / Magnetism
Ground of Being
Spirituality
Wholeness and the Whole-I-Spirit
Conscious Creation
Co-Creation
The Thought-Become Process

Please start ReThinking these things Now
So as to be properly prepared

———————————————

<u>The Internet As God</u>

Where
Exactly
Is
The Internet
?

Hoboken?
Toledo?
Paducah?
Brussels?
Moscow?
Beijing?

Yes!
It
Is Everywhere
At Once
!

It is Everywhere
We Are

It is In the Air
We Breathe

We Walk Through
Its Substance
Unaware –
Yet It Is There

It Is Here
Now

———————

Perspective

To Personify God
Does incredible Injustice to the Great Mystery
Which is Source and Sustenance
to
All that Are

We cannot even begin to understand the Great Mystery
by Pretending that It is Something Else
by Turning the Infinite into something we can Imagine
Something we Think we could Face

We try to make God small
Because We *feel* small

Would it not be Better to Teach our Children
To Gaze into the Night Sky and Say:
"All of This is God."
"All of This is Me."
"All is One."

All Is One

And the Smallest Portion
Contains
The Whole

O-to the 3ʳᵈ Power

All Powerful
The very Source of
All Power

All Knowing
All *Intended* to Know
The smallest grain of sand
The smallest cell within our bodies
Every atom
Each particle
All Knowing

All Known
All Cherished within
This Ocean of Great Mystery

The One Self

Solid Thinking

Think Your Body is Solid?
You're Wrong!

Wind – just Air Moving over Rock
Will Erode a Mountain
Into Dust!
That is a Scientific Fact

And we have This scientific fact:
One Hundred *Trillion* Neutrinos
Pass Through Our Bodies
Every **Second** of Every **Minute** of Every **Day**
One Hundred Trillion –

That's a 1 with Fourteen Zeros after it
100,000,000,000,000
Per Second
Six *Quadrillion* per Minute
Yet We do not even Notice

Try That with a Solid Body –

———————

Profound Universal Truth #19

Nothing
Really
Matters

———————

That Which Matters

Behold this Block of Steel
Lift it – Feel the
Weight
Let your fingers
Caress
The Flawless Surface

But Look, Closer
There Are
Very Small
Irregularities
and
Closer Still
Microscopic Canyons
Like
Great Rifts –
Gaping *Openness*
Within this
Not-So-Solid Metal

And Closer Still
the *Openness*
the *Emptiness*
Seems to Grow
Until
you can *See*
the Empty Space
Is
Greater in Size
Than the Molecules Themselves

At the Atomic Level
It is almost as if
you *were* Gazing into the Emptiness of Space
And Closer again –
to Gaze upon
the Subatomic World
To Examine the Particles
Which Build this Universe

At Last We *See* that there
*Is **Nothing***
To See
there is
*No **T**hing*
to see

It is only a **Vibrating**
Cluster
of *E*nergy
Pulsing
Ever Moving
Ever
Changing

At Last We See
there
IS
No **M**atter
IN
That *which*
Matters

Profound Universal Truth #39

Thou art It
It art Thee
The Universe is just a bunch of It, you See!

<u>EMOTIONALLY</u>

The Evidence is All Around Us
All the Time
And it really takes No Great Effort to Grasp the Science –
Not necessarily the Formulas
But the Basic Logic of It

A Good Book or Two
Or just a couple of hours with
"What the Bleep Do We Know?"
(What a Great Movie!)

Intellectually
It's Easy Enough to Understand

Emotionally
It's quite a Different Story

"Baby, I Know Your Energy is The Same
As My Energy – But, Damn it Feels Good
When you Wrap those Electrons
Around my Protons
And your Molecules slide down my..."

Well, you get the Idea –
Emotionally
It's quite a Different Story

———————————

<u>FAIRNESS</u>

We need to get rid of our Old Ideas about
GOD
Especially the Idea that God is a Done-Deal
"Finished"
In some Kindergarten concept of "Perfection"

*But, **"God Is
Always Was and
Always Will Be!"***

No Argument There – But that Don't mean He's
"DONE"
Think about yourself…

I've been around better than a half century.
Now, I Am.
I Was.
And I sure as hell plan on Will Be!
But, I Ain't Done!

I am not Now what I Was
And I am not Now what I Will Be
It's a Process…
A Continuing Evolution
That's the Way of Life –
Big or Little doesn't matter

If we accept that we ARE made in the Image and Likeness –
Can't we give God
the Same Freedom we have?
Can't we accept that God
is
Growing
Learning
Evolving
Expanding
?
That *is* the Way of Life.
And seein' as how God *is*
the SOURCE of All Life…
It just seems more
Fair
If it goes Both ways…

_____

EVOLUTION

We are Evolving
Because
God is Evolving
Because
We are Evolving
Because
God is Evolving

This is *NOT* Circular-Logic
This *IS*
Spiraling Truth
Great Spirals of Evolution
Twisting through Each Other
Blending
Expanding
In every Direction
In every Dimension
Constantly Creating new
Spirals of Consciousness
Evolving
In every Direction
In every Dimension
Intertwining Again and Again and Again
Creating
Evolving
Creating Anew
Evolving Anew

It is Happening Right Now!

Profound Universal Truth #6

*God Created
the Universe
Out of
Sheer Curiosity*

The New God

The *Old* Idea of God is – God as King
The Majestic Ruler
The Final Judge

And This God
Demands our Fealty
And our Unquestioning Service
In His Name
This God is the Beneficent Dictator

We have even Applied this Model
To the Natural World
Viewing the Queen Ant and Queen Bee As
Beneficent Dictators
Who Demand Loyalty and Service
Of Each Subject

We have seen them as Tiny Omniscient Creatures
Who Act by Secret Inner Knowledge
Of What the Colony
Will Need
But Science has Learned
This Model is Completely Wrong!

The Queen does Not Dictate
Does Not Demand

The Queen is The Source –
Literal Mother of All
Yet She only *Responds*
To the Will of the Colony

When the *Colony* Realizes
The Need for More
Nursemaids
Workers
Foragers
Warriors
Then Word is Sent to the Queen

Now Is The *Power* of the Queen –
Now She Will Change
The Very Nature of the Egg
Within Her Womb
To Meet this New Requirement

She *Is* Eternal Source
She *Is* Limitless Potential
but
She is *Not* Liege
She is *Not* Dictator

She Is only the *Willing Servant*
Of Her Children
Ever Doing Their Bidding
Without Question
Without Judgment

So it Is with the Real God

This Should Be
The New Idea of God:

The Queen God
Always Our Source
Ever Willing to Do Our Bidding

Without Question
Without Judgment

To All My Atheist Friends,

I Do-Not-Believe in the Same God
Which You Do-Not-Believe In.

Love to All,

God

Job Assignments

We need to get rid of the Idea
That God is The Boss
God is Not the Boss!

We Are

But it's Better
To just Junk the Whole Concept Of
Boss
We are Equal Partners with God
We just have Different
Job Descriptions

God Imagined Us
As Being Totally Free
With All the Universe
At Our Disposal

Anything
Absolutely Anything
Ours for the Asking
Our Job is the Asking

We supply the Instructions
God does the Work

…Works for Me…

Working Arrangement

(A Musical Tribute to Reality)

♪♪ La La – La La!
God works for Me-e
God works for Me-e

La La – La La!
And who could Ask
For a Better
La La – La La!
Em-ployee-ee
? ♪♪

<u>DENSITY</u>

I Create
My Own Reality
You Create
Your Own Reality

She Creates
Her Own Reality
He Creates
His Own Reality

We Each Create Our Own Realities

I wonder How Many Times I've
Heard
Read
Felt
Remembered
This Most Basic Truth
And
I Still Didn't Get It!

But plain ol' Garden Variety Logic Says It's So –

Man ("Kind" for the Politically-Correct)
was Given Free Will
So –
Of Course We Create Our Own Realities!

If you gots Free Will
Shit Don't Happen To You –
'les You Let It!

It's the Only Way It Can Be…

———————————

<u>The Truth Is Out There</u>

"As Ye Sow – So shall Ye Reap"
"Garbage In – Garbage Out"
(GIGO)

"Birds of a Feather..."
"What goes around – comes around"
"It's a Self-Fulfilling-Prophecy"

"Attitude makes All the Difference"
"It's not the cards you're Dealt –
it's how you Play them"

"Life is What You Make It –
Always has been
Always will be"

"As Ye Believe – So shall it be Done Unto Thee"

There are At Least
Four thousand, seven hundred twelve
Different Ways
To describe the Truth
And only One Way to Hear It –
Our Hearts Know the Truth

"Listen to Your Heart"

————————————

Cogs or Gods

It really boils down
To One of Two choices…
We are Either
Cogs
or
Gods

Nothing *In-Between* Really Works

We are Cogs –
Slaves to some unknown, accidental Machine
Out of Control
Having NO SAY in our own Lives
Nothing
Nothing
Nothing
Has, Can, or Ever Will
Make One Bit of Difference!

Or
We are Gods –
Gods
Who have Dreamt Cities
Languages
Cultures
Rituals
Sciences
Spaceships

We are Gods –
Awakening to our Oneness
Awakening to our Power
Awakening to our Responsibility
Awakening to our Freedom

It Really
can be
Only
One

———

<u>THOU ART GOD</u>

Thou Art God
WOW!
What a Concept!

Kinda goes to your head when you Realize – *YOU*
Really *Are* the Center of the Universe
(OK – the Center of *Your* Universe, but still…)
You Are God
Looking at the Universe through *Your* Eyes
Feeling the Universe through *Your* Skin
Your Emotions

No One Else has Your *Perspective*
No One Else Can Offer
This *Gift* to God

This is our Value
Far beyond Gold or Diamonds
This is our Worth
Undeniable
Everything We Do
Think
Feel
Anything we can Imagine
Everything we Experience in Any Way

Is Given onto God
For We are One with God
Inseparable –

Priest or Whore
Hero or Victim
Architect or Assassin
Willingly or Unwillingly
Knowingly or Unknowingly
Your Life
IS
A Dedication to God

Thou Art God

…WOW…

———————

<u>Profound Universal Truth #7</u>

God is an Experience-Junkie

<u>EveryThink in the World</u>

We need to Really *Get* This
The Idea – the Fact – that *We*
Control
The World that We See
The World that We Experience

That All the Forms
Occupying Space
Existing in Time
Are
Fluid
Mutable
And they
Become
Whatever We Expect them to Be

We Are the Controllers
The Directors
The Painters of our own Worldscapes

Our Thoughts
Our Beliefs
Our Emotions
Our Expectations
Are the Paints and Brushes we Use to Create

They are the Chisel and Hammer
That Carve our Life

We need to Really *Get* This
We need to Stop thinking about
the Things of the World
As Things *Out There*

We need to Realize
We have Created
EveryThink in Our World

Thought-Becomes

There is a Process – A Formula to Living
That needs to be Understood:

The Process of Becoming

Thoughts are Offered to us by the Universe –
Ours for the Choosing
And once we Choose
Once we *Name It Ours*
So It Is!

And as we Attend to this new addition to our Self
Our *Attending* gives Strength and Will
It is the Will to Be!
And when it is Strong Enough
It *Becomes*

It Manifests in Full-Blown 3-D
That we may examine in more depth, this
Thought-Become

That we may experience
The Physical Textures
The Emotional Resonance
of
This *Thought-Become*

Every Thing, Every Thing, Every Thing!
IS
A Thought-Become

We are the *Thought-Becoming's* of God
That *Great Mystery* may Experience *ItSelf*
In Physical Texture
In Emotional Resonance

As our very Life is a Gift *from* God
Our *Thought-Becomes* are Each One
Our Gifts *to* God

Thoughts are Offered to us by the Universe –
Ours for the Choosing

And the Thoughts we may Choose
Are
Limitless

———

DREAMERS

We are Created to Dream
To Imagine
Things Which are Not in Our World
To Dream of a Different World
To Imagine a Different Life

As Children We Do This
Effortlessly
Naturally
Never Doubting the Possibility of *That Reality*

We All Dream of Flying
Until We are Told – That is Only a Dream
And Then We Doubt
And Rarely again will We Dream of Flying

And as We grow older We are Taught
Dreams of Freedom
Dreams of Happiness
Dreams of Love, of Peace
Dreams of a Better Way
Are Unrealistic, Unattainable

We are Taught that Dreaming – Especially "Day-Dreaming"
Is a Waste of Time
We are even Taught that it is Sin
That God will Punish Us

Why would *Any* God Punish Us
For Doing what He Created Us to Do?
Why should *Anyone Else?*

The Avatars, The Teachers of Truth, The Great Entrepreneurs
All Tell Us
"Follow your Dream"
"Visualize; Imagine your Dream"
"If you can Imagine It, you can Do It"

To Imagine –
To Dream of That Which is Not Yet
Is How we Tell the Universe
What We Want
It is How We Create

We are Created to Dream –
We are Born to Live Our Dreams!

Chapter Two

The Way It Is

"Truths and roses have thorns about them."
Henry David Thoreau

Part one – the way we think it is

The Accidental Universe

The Universe is nothing more than a Cosmic Accident
These elements just happened to mix with Those elements
to Accidentally create Life

And after those initial accidents
Then the various forms of Life stabilized
So that the Same Accident which created them
Would create their Children
And then another Accident occurred
Which created Another Life Form which would Be
Food for the First Life Form
And That Accident stabilized
And so on and so forth

It's all Just an Accident – Mechanical Momentum
Not Mystic Miracle
Intelligence itself is an Illusion
It's just electro-chemical Stimulus and Response
Emotion is the same thing
It's all Meaningless Mechanics
Just an Accident that Happened

Just because Every Life Form has a Place and a Purpose
And Every Life Form fits into One Inseparable Ecology
And all the Plants fit with all the Animals
And all the Plants and all the Animals
Fit with All the Minerals
And just because Life *Abounds* in every Conceivable Place
And in every *Inconceivable* Place
It's Still Just a Meaningless Accident
Senseless Mechanical Behavior –
God is just the way that weak-minded people
Try to Cope with the Meaninglessness of it All
They just don't want to Face the Facts!
They can't Deal with Reality!

*(? No – I'm not chewing gum, or tobacco. That's my Tongue in my Cheek –
I saw you nodding your head, so I thought I'd throw in a visual-aid.)*

The Way We Think It Is

I think most of us
Believe
That there is some kind of Preordained Path
Or Destiny
Or at least some kind of Momentum
That keeps the World Running

Some Believe their part in Life's Great Play
Is to Fight the Battle of Good vs Evil

Others Believe
We are no more than Pawns
Being Played by the Powers That Be
With No Will of Our Own

Some Believe
Life is just a Game of Chance
That Luck Alone steers Our Course
Others Believe
All Is Fate –
Written in Tablets of Stone Long Before our Births

Still Others Believe
Life has No Meaning
We are just Biological
Accidents
Driven by Instinct Alone
And Consciousness Itself is only Illusion
And Delusion!

Many Believe
Life Itself is a Great Struggle
A Challenge to be Met with All Strength and All Courage

And the *Reality*
Is more akin to an old TV commercial
"Stop – You're *All* Right."

We Each Create the World
As We Believe
The World Is

———————

This is Not A Test

Some say that our
Life's Journey
Is a Series of Lessons that
Must be Learned
To Purify the Soul
To Prepare the Soul for
The Great Test
Final Judgment

I say Phooey!
(I guess I'm feeling Polite at the moment…)

LIFE
IS
NOT A TEST
!

Life is *Living*
Life is *Joy*
and
Sorrow
and
Mystery
and
Wonder

Yes, Life *Has* Lessons
We can indeed *Learn* from our Journeys
But there is no Great Syllabus in the Sky
There is no Predetermined Schedule of Classes

I Believe that We Should Learn to be Gentler
With Ourselves
With Each Other
With the Earth
And the Other Lives
Who Share our planet

I Believe that We Should Become More
Aware of Our Spiritual Self
I Believe that This
Is Better
For the Individual
For the Species
For the World
For the Universe Itself!

But there *Are*
No Classes
No Tests to Pass
No Diplomas to Earn

Some say that Mankind has A *Destiny*!
I Believe that Fate
and
Free Will
are
Mutually Exclusive!
By Definition
By Reality
By God!

I Believe that
Humanity
Has a *Goal* –
But it is more of a
Direction-of-Evolution
than a
Preordained-Destination
(Complete with Map Coordinates and Deadline)

I Believe that
We are Still Free to
Blow-It!
But I have Great Faith in Us
As Individuals
As a Species

We are Still Free to
Do-It-Right!

Eternal Question / Cosmic Answer

Why are we Here?
What is the Meaning of Life?
We keep Asking these questions –
And the Answers are Always the Same:

We are Here
Because We Want to be Here
The Meaning of Life Is
The Living of Life
The Loving of Life

I heard my Favorite again, a few days ago –
We are Here
To Play!

The Answers are Always the Same:
Yet We Hear them
And almost immediately
Forget them

We have Forgotten
How to Live
How to Play
We've let Ourselves Become
The Slave of Fears
And the Most Terrible Master:
"NOT ENOUGH"

We Tremble and Toil
In something which is Much Less than Living
And "play" in that World of Fear
Is only Distraction
A Temporary bandage for a Wounded Soul

LIFE IS MEANT TO BE JOYOUS!

We come Here to be
COSMIC–OTTERS
Swimming Fearlessly through
Great Rivers of Abundance
Playing Freely
With *Endless* Realities
Creating New Worlds
Creating New Eternities
CREATING!
PLAYING!
THAT Is
Our Reason for Being!

The Universe IS Endless Bounty
Ours for the Asking!
Ours to Use
Any Way We Choose

———————————

__The Devil Made Me Do It__

There are Always
Seeming Reasons
The great multitude of circumstances
Outside Ourselves
Beyond Our Control

And Each and Every Reason
Each Person
Every Thing
Seen in That Light
IS
Self-Delusion
of the
Greatest Order!

There is No Force
No External Power
No Outside Agency –
Natural or Contrived
Period!

We
Are What Happens
To
Us
Period!

There is No Devil
Making Us Do Anything
Period!

———————

The Why of Now

"God, what a Life –
If you can call This, Life!"

Well, it Is – *Life*
For You
For Me
For Everyone

We All have our share of Troubles
And
Things we Don't Like
And
We Easily become Convinced
This *is* the Way it Is

Yet We Each
Live
The Life We Choose

We All have our Share of Troubles
And
Things we Don't Like
But Our Troubles
Are the Result of our Own Thoughts
Or more precisely
Our Miss-thoughts
The Result of Unchecked Thoughts
And Emotions
This is The *Why* of *Now*

We Each Live the Life
We Choose

Whether We Know It
Or Not

God Is A Delicate Balance

God is a Delicate Balance –

The Perfect Controlled Precision
     of an Olympic High Diver
        As he twists through the Air
     Into the Water

       The Perfect Abandon
    of a Happy Drunk
    As he rolls and bounces
  and Laughs
      Down the side of a Mountain

And Both have Flawless Landings
    10pts   10pts

Thou Art God

God is a Delicate Balance –
     A coin placed on edge atop a House of Cards
   On a Tray
      Being Carried Across a Very Large Room
     Filled with People

      Will it Fall?
      Will it Hold?

Thou Art God

Choose!

————

<u>This Is Why</u>

There is this One-Question
People (usually atheists or agnostics –
but certainly Not Limited to the "Non-Believer")
Ask:
If there Is a God –
Then Why do Bad Things
Happen to Good People
?

Ignoring the Obvious
What Is Good / What Is Bad Quandary
The Real Reason is *Still:*
They Have Created
Their Own Reality

And, Of Course No One *WANTS* Disease, War, Poverty, Etc, Etc,
And No One Creates this shit
Consciously

Yet Each and Every Experience has been Invited

It is Invited through
Our Thoughts OF It
It is Invited through
Our Belief IN It
It is Invited through
Our Emotions ABOUT It
Hurried Along by Worry and Fear

Just as the *Experiences-Wanted*
Are *Held at Bay* By Our Own Doubts –
Doubt of our Worthiness
Doubt of our Deservedness
Doubt of our own Power
Doubt even of *The Possibility*

Yet This Truth Is Not New!
It has been Taught
Time and Again
Through Century after Century
Through All the Millennia of History
And Beyond

The Power to Choose Our Own Reality
Has Always
Is Now and
Will Ever
Be
Within Each of Us

This Is the Way It Really Is!

So – There it is, in a Nutshell
"Bad" Things Happen
To "Good" People
BECAUSE
They are Not Listening to the Teachers!

Because they Don't *Believe*
That *Thoughts* Make Any Difference
That *Emotions* and *Feelings*
Make Any Difference

Because they Don't *Believe*
Change is Possible
Because they Don't *Believe*
They are Worthy
They Don't Believe
– *Really Believe* –

They Are Children of the Universe
Children of God

Profound Universal Truth #58

Whether You Believe it or Not –
Whether You Like it or Not –
You Are STILL God.

Part two – the way it really is

<u>The Way It Is</u>

Our Beliefs are the Eyes Which See Our World –

We can only See the World
We *Believe* Exists
If someone tells us –
"This is the way the world Is – Look!"
Our Eyes will be Blind

We can only See what we Believe

If Other-ness is presented to us –
Our Beliefs will
Twist and Turn the World –
Until we See what we Expect to See

Our Beliefs are The Eyes which See Our World –

Our World Is the Way It Is
Because
We Believe that That Is the Way It Is

That does not mean that we are Wrong
OR
That we are Right

And That <u>Is</u>
The Way It Is!

To Change Our World
We need to *Believe* that

There Is
More
Than Meets the Eye

———————

The Reality of Self

We are *In*
This World
But
Not *Of*
This World
Born of This Earth
Formed
From the Very Flesh
of Our Mother
Yet This *Form*
Is but
A *Lens*
Which *Focuses Upon*
The Flesh and the Forms of
This World
We are Not This Form
We Are Not
Contained-In
This Form
Anymore than our Little Fingers
Contain
The Whole of our Bodies
We
Are Not
Bound to this
Single Focus

We
Are
Infinite!

Through this *Finite Lens*
We View this World
With
Infinite Mind
Through this Finite Flesh
We Create this World
With
Infinite Possibilities

We Are Limitless!

Life Is

Life Is
What You Believe
It Is

What do you Believe?

Life Is
What You Believe
It Is

Is Life Easy?

Life Is
What You Believe
It Is

Is Life Good?

Life Is
What You Believe
It Is

Is Life Limitless
In Its Abundance and Freedom?

Life Is
What You Believe
It Is

What do *You* Believe?

—————————

48

Profound Universal Truth #1

Eagle

An

When you Believe

As

That

Soar

you are

not

Bound

can

to the

You

Earth

As

A

STONE
_____

BELIEFS

"As ye Believe – so shall it be Done unto thee"

Our Beliefs are the Censors of our Life
Even Memory is Censored
Filtered Through our Beliefs
Until All Events
Conform to the Shape of our Current Belief

Our Beliefs are the Sensors of our Life
Ever Seeking More Proof that We are Right
That This is Truth

And *Whatever* the Belief
The Universe will supply Ample Proof
That THIS Belief
IS Truth
Or
That Another's Belief Is Not Truth

Yet Beliefs Are Not Truth

Beliefs Are only Ideas
In which we have Invested Emotion
They are only Ideas
We *Think* Are Truth

They are only Ideas
Which may be Exchanged
For Better Ideas

We can each Choose New Ideas

And if we are Willing to Invest Positive
Emotions
Into this New Idea
Then we can make This our New and Better Belief
This Will Be Our New Truth

We may Start
By Choosing to Believe that
The *Possibility of Change*
May *Possibly*
Be Truth

_____

<u>NOT</u>

The Rich Get Richer
It Takes Money to Make Money

Everybody is Out For Themselves
It's a Dog Eat Dog World

People are all Greedy
People always try to Take Advantage
of Other People –
Situations

Everybody is out to Get All They Can
Regardless of How
Or Who Gets Hurt

You Can't Trust Anyone
People never tell the Truth
Everyone is a Liar

Everybody Gets Old
Everybody Gets Sick

There is Never Enough
There is Only So Much to Go Around
Get it while you Can

The World is a Dangerous Place
You Never Know What's Going to Happen Next
People have Accidents All the Time

The World is Filled with Germs
Bacteria
Viruses
Diseases Keep Getting Worse

The World is Filled with Lunatics
Crazy People
Bad People

It Keeps getting Harder to Make a Living
To Make Ends Meet

The Preceding are *Just* Beliefs –
The Preceding are *NOT* Beneficial Beliefs!

———————————

We Are All Free

I am Free
You are Free
We are All Free
To Accept the World as Others Say It Is

We are Free to See the World as We Believe It Is
(There are more than Two Sides to *This Coin*!)
We Are All Free
We are Free to Live as We Think We Should

We are Free to take the Side of Right
In
Right versus Wrong
We are Free to *See* that Right and Wrong
Are like the Leaves of Autumn
No Two are Exactly the Same Color
And no One Color
Is Truer than Another

We are Free to Have a Favorite Color
And We are Free to Choose Another
We Are All Free

We are Free to Live
By these Proper Rules
By these Paper Rules

We are Free to See
The Rules of Others
May be True for Them
Or Were, in some Distant When

We are Free to Abandon All the Should's and Ought's
We are Free to Think Our Own Thoughts

We are Free to Follow the Calling of Our Hearts
We Are All Free
He and She and
You and Me

I Choose This Freedom
And My Heart
Soars In Ecstasy

––––––––––––

Secular Freedom

Let's leave *God* out of it –
No Mention
No Thought
No Nuttin'

If we just observe the people around us
People we encounter
People we see and hear on a regular basis
We can only come to one conclusion
About the way
Life Works:

We Are Self-Fulfilling Prophecies

People will Tell you their Future
Listen and Watch
They will All teach you
They will tell you
Exactly What they Want
And in the Same Breath
Tell you Exactly
Why *They* will *Never*
Have It
Or Do It
Or Be It

But every so often we get to witness
The Miracle Workers
These are the people who tell you Exactly
What they Want
What they are going to
Have
Or Do
Or Be

And if you Ask these Wise Ones
How this will Happen
They will unanimously answer:
"I don't Know – but it Will!"
And it Does
And they Do

Because they Believe it Will
Because they Believe in Themselves
Just as those who Believe in their own Failure
Will Always
Achieve their own Failure

We Are Self-Fulfilling Prophecies

We Create Our Own Lives
Our Own Experiences
Through Our Beliefs

What we Believe
IS
What we
Get!

Listen to those around you –
Watch their lives
Listen to the *Beliefs*
You
Think and Speak
Look at your own life

We Are Self-Fulfilling Prophecies

Profound Universal Truth #2

If your Belief is In Any Way
Limiting, Restricting, Demanding –
It is Not Yet Truth

Profound Universal Truth #52

You are Not what you Tell the World you are –
You Are what you Tell your Self you are.

Seeing It In Others

It is So Much Easier
to Note this
to Track these Patterns
to See
the Almost Instantaneous Effect
that Thought-Habits Produce

When We Gaze upon the Lives of Others

We can So Clearly See the
Self-Contradictory Statements
The Conflicted Intentions
The Opposing Beliefs

When We Gaze upon the Lives of Others

We See the Tug-of-War
Between Faith and Fear
Between Desire and Shame
Between Worth and Worthlessness
It is On Display for All to See

When We Gaze upon the Lives of Others

We can Feel the Emotions
Swirling
Twisting Without
Twisting Within

We See
We Feel
And there is Something – Some Part – Within the Self
That Knows
They Have Done This To Themselves

When We Gaze upon the Lives of Others

There is Some Part of Us that Recognizes
We are All
Doing This To Ourselves

We Are What Happens to Us

————————

Part three – the process of living

<u>Wanting</u>

There Is
No Right
No Wrong
There Only
IS

There is Nothing *Wrong*
In
Wanting
And there is Nothing *Wrong*
In
Having
But Wanting and Having are Not Our Rights
They Are
Our Purpose
Our Reason For
Being

When We are *Wanting*
We are *In the Image of Our Creator*
When We are *Having*
We are *In the Likeness*

We Are the Children of the Universe
and
We Can Only
Be
What We Are!

––––––––––

<u>Easy Living</u>

Abundance is our Birth-Right
Our
Inheritance from the Universe

We are *meant* to be the Spoiled Children of the Cosmos
Never to be Denied
Or even Limited
In Any Way

Ask and it Shall be Given!

Abundant Affluence
IS
Our Natural State of Being

There is Always Enough for Everyone
Now and Forever
There is Always Enough

Ask and it Shall be Given!

Ask
And
It Shall Be Given...

Living just doesn't get any Easier than
THIS
!

<u>ABUNDANCE</u>

So many people think of Abundance as sort of a
Squirrel-Thing
Something you have to Save
Hoard
Hide Away

Something that Some Have
And Others Don't

That is Not Abundance

That is the Coin-of-Lack:
One side
Has
One side
Has Not

True Abundance is
Always
More than Enough
True Abundance is
The Natural State of the Universe

True Abundance is
The Current State of the Universe
Our Own World Included

It was Not a Miracle
When Jesus took a few
Loaves of Bread and some Fish
And Fed Thousands
With Leftovers!

It was True Abundance in Action

Jesus *Knew* – with Faith we can scarce Imagine –
He Knew
The Universe *IS* Abundance Itself
It was His *Intent* to Feed Everyone –
He simply *Allowed* the Flow of Abundance

This is how Life is
Supposed to Be

This is how Life IS

If We will Allow It

————————

If ever Doubtest thee
Abundance
Then gaze upon thine own Street
On Trash Day

THOUGHTS

"Thoughts" just "Are"
They Exist – Complete and Independent of Us
Flying through the Universe Faster Than Light
They are Everywhere –

Sometimes I believe Quantum Physicists will
Proclaim "Thoughts"
As the "Ultimate Particle"
The Basis of All Form

Each Particle Ready to Serve Us as We Would Choose

Unique to a Single Person
Or Shared by Millions
"Thoughts"
Are Working Together
To *Form* the World we Know

Yet a Single Thought
Can Change the Universe

It Does!

Thoughts on Thoughts

"Thought" – It's What the Mind –"Does"

We sit in front of a Mental Screen
Watching this endless Parade of Thoughts
Choosing –
"Ooh – I *Like* That One!"
"No – I think I'll *Pass* on That One…"

The most rudimentary of self examination
Will convince most of us That
We Do Not "Make Up" Thoughts
They just Come to Us –

The Strange Single Thought
The Train of Thought
Happy Thoughts
Sad Thoughts
Loving Thoughts
Hurtful Thoughts

Thoughts are the Breath of the Mind

And Like-Thoughts gather together into Waves
That Wash Over Us

By Our Choosing –
Frolicking like Dolphins
Or
Threatening As a School of Sharks
But Always
By Our Choice

Always Are We Free to Choose
Always Are We Free to Refuse
And the Thoughts we Choose
Will Determine the Life we Live

This is Scientific Fact –
"Thoughts"
Actually Change the Physical Structures
Of our Brains
And our Bodies

This is Scientific Fact –
"Thoughts"
Influence the Physical World around us

This is Scientific Fact –
"Thoughts"
Can Pre-Determine the Outcome of Future Events

This is Scientific Fact –
"Thoughts"
Are Forming the World We Know

"Thoughts"
Are Doing That Right Now –

Watch Them!

———————

<u>The Good, the Bad, and the Ugly</u>

Good Thoughts
Bad Thoughts
That is Value Judgment only
ALL IS

A single Thought will have
Little or
No Effect –
It is only the
Patterns of Thought
The *Repetition* of the Same Thought
The *Same Type* of Thought
Which *Magnetizes the Universe*

A Thought is not even Our Own
Until We Claim it So
No one Forces Thoughts into Us –

We are not Thought-Sausages!

We Draw Thoughts To Us
With our Beliefs and our Emotions –
Like unto Like
And those Thoughts which We Claim
As Our Own
Will then be Free To
Manifest
Into *Our Reality*

We are Always
Free
To Choose New Thoughts

They are only Thoughts

———————

<u>Profound Universal Truth #27</u>

A Thought may Appear
To come Unbidden –
But it will only Stay
If Invited!

———————

Part four – time for a reality check

<u>TIME</u>

The Universe Paints
This "Background"
With Broad
Slow
Sweeping Cycles

Yet we Stand Transfixed
As we Peer
Ever Closer
Ever Smaller

The Seasons
Become Months
Months   Days

Even the Hours
No longer Flow
Freely
But are Crippled into Minutes
Each Minute
Denied Uniqueness and Totality

Now we Attack the Seconds
Cutting
Cutting
As if a Fraction of a Nanosecond
Will
Reveal
The Infinite Expanse
of
N   O   W

We sit in this Self-Made Prison
Watching the Seconds Pass
Waiting for Life to
Arrive

———————

Timeless Truth

So many live *Not for Today*
But give themselves away to Memories
of Long Gone Today's
Or waste their energies
Worrying about Tomorrows
That need never become a Single Today

"Yesterday"
Is only a way to speak of Memories
"Tomorrow"
Is only a way to speak of Hope and Desire
Neither is Real

You cannot Undo
You cannot Redo
Even the Last Moment
It is No More
You cannot Eat Tomorrow's
Food
Nor Drink Tomorrow's Wine
But Food and Drink are before you Now
Rejoice in This Feast

Let the Joy and Beauty of the Past
Inspire you
and Give Direction
Let the Grief and Shame
Give you Strength and Resolve

But if you wish to *Truly Live*
There is only
NOW
And our Lives are Built of
Billions and Billions of
NOWs

There is No Beginning to
NOW
There is No Ending to
NOW

Eternity is NOW

<u>NOW</u>

Some Scientists will study Anything
Which *has* lead to some Amazing Stuff
Sometimes pretty Useless – But still Amazing

Some research makes one wonder
Why Anyone would waste their time – this is Common Sense!
Everyone Knows this Already!

But, what the Hell – Now it's
Scientifically Proven

But I just heard about one that caught my attention:
How Long Is "Now"?

After all, we're told to "Live in the Now"
"Now is All we Have"
"Now is the Point of All Power"
So
How Long IS "NOW"?

It turns out
That to the Human Brain
NOW
Lasts Five Seconds.

That's the whole duration of Now – just
Five Seconds
When the Sixth second arrives, second One is
In the Past!

Not a Lot of Time…
Might as well think of Something Nice
Something that makes you Smile
Makes you Feel Good

Might as well be Grateful for what you Have
NOW

The Eternal NOW is only Five Seconds long...

Do you want to Waste Eternity
Bitchin' and Moanin'
?

NOT-LIVING

Focused on Tomorrow
or The Day after That –
Worrying about The Unknown Future
is
Not-Living

Worry for the Future
Can Create
Self-Fulfilling Prophesies of Doom

Focus upon the Days Gone Forever
Or upon
Some Act now Written Indelibly in Time
is
Not-Living

Dragging our Past with us
Like a Dead Siamese-Twin
Makes a poor Excuse for Life

Even the Joys of the Past
Are but Memory to be Cherished
Not Worshipped
This Too
is
Not-Living

Regret over the Past
Will Not Undo It
Anger about the Past
Will Not Heal Any Wounds
Regret and Anger
are
Not-Living

In all the Billions of Years the Living-Earth has Circled the Sun
And all the Billions of Years
Still to come
Living
Exists Only In The Now

Living
Exists Only Here

Ram Dass, Forgive Them

It's close to the end of August
And I'm hearing these Comments
"Autumn is Here"
"Now that it's Fall"

I Know it's Close –
But we have Already had Halloween Decorations
and Candies in the Stores for
the last Two Weeks!

Richard Alpert* must be Rolling in his Grave!
Science be talkin' 'bout
Five Seconds
These People can't even Cope with
Today
As in Twenty-Four Hours

Ram Dass, Forgive Them –
For They Know Not
When They Are

---

*Richard Alpert changed his name to Ram Dass, and at the time of this writing, "both" are alive and well.

Great Titles In History #28

BE HERE THEN
or
How to Completely Miss Your Life
Minute by Minute

ReIncarNation

♪♪We have All been Here Before♪♪

So says the Song
All the Great Teachers
All the Discorporate Entities
Most all the Mystics
And a Lot of Legends –
Makes ya think, Maybe it's True

Personally, I think it Is True
But I also Know –
It doesn't Make Any Difference

The Point
of Pointing to Reincarnation
Is
To Establish in the Mind
To Recognize in the Heart
That
We are All Part of the *Great Being*
Which Is
Everything
Has Always Been
Everything
And Will Always
Be
Everything
There are No New Souls
Just as
There are No Old Souls

We All
Are
As We Have Always Been

We are All Children of
The Eternal Mystery
and
We
Are
HERE NOW

———

When The World Began

I Know
The Exact Day
The World
Began –

It was the 16th Day of March
In the Year of Our Lord Nineteen Hundred and Forty Nine
(I Know – the Date *is* Very Different
In the Chinese and the Mayan Calendars)
But That's the Exact Day
The World Began –
The Day I Arrived!

So, You're probably Thinking –
"Well if you Want
to look at it That Way –
Then the World began on May 6th,
or July 9th –
Whatever someone's Birthday is…"
Exactly!

Give the Lady a Cigar!
Flowers for the Gentleman!

The World Is Born Anew
Each Moment
of
Each Day

The World Is Being Born
This Very Instant
Anew
Again
Forever
And Forever
Anew
As
It
Always
Has and Will
The World
Begins With Each of Us

The World
Begins
NOW
!

Eternity on a Silver Platter

Everyone Wants Eternal Life
Until it's Handed to them
Here!
This is It!
This IS Eternal Life:
Now
This is All you Have
This is All you can *ever* Have:
Now

But it IS Never Ending
And
It IS your Place of Power
It IS the Well Spring of
All the Now's to come

It IS the Very Heart
of
Life –

This IS Eternity
NOW
What are you going to
DO
with it
?

Profound Universal Truth #13

In the Vastness of the Eternal Now
Lies the Future of your Dreams

Be Here Now

Chapter Three

Meanwhile, Back at the Ranch

"Life goes on within you and without you…"
The Beatles

The preceding Chapters and those which follow this present segment, deal primarily with my *interpretation* of very ancient Truths – giving only a New Perspective. This Chapter is an effort to share the Impact of these Truths in My Life. It is an effort to show that making these Truths a Real Part of our Life, making them the Basis of our Life, is both the Absolutely Simplest Thing in the World and as Difficult as conquering Mt. Everest.

At least that is the way I see it right now, so that pretty much makes it My Reality…

Part one – the world as I see it

The Night Louisville Went Crazy
(In Three Part Harmony)

Part One

OK – There *is* a line of Strong Thunderstorms
Heading our way
(Tornado Watch in Effect)
This *has* happened a few
Tens-of-Thousands of Times Before

Reported Hail –
Some the Size of Golf balls
This Too is *not* an Unknown Phenomenon

So – WHY have our two "Leading" Television Stations
Suddenly Decided
This Storm Is a
Major Media Event
?

They Both pre-empt a
Full Night of Network Programming
(And in No Defense of the Boob-Tube –
The Networks' Top Shows –
Heavy Water Cooler Stuff!)
To Report:
That No Tornados Ever Formed
(OK – *maybe* One that *didn't* Touch Down)

To Report:
Although the Rate of Rainfall *is Over 4" per Hour*
The Storms are moving Too Fast
To create *Any* Risk of Flooding
– *Anywhere* –

And after Three Hours of "Updates"
Reporting the same
Non-Event
They are *Still* telling people to Wrap themselves in Blankets
"Be Sure to Cover your Head..."
And
"Hide in your Safe-place!"

I think I'll go Outside
Watch the "Storm" for a while
Enjoy a Smoke

Part Two

80 mph Wind Gusts
Inch-and-a-half Hail Stones
Tornado Warnings
Nasty Threats!

But the Reality is
Most of Metro-Louisville had
Some Rain

The Reality is
Most of the towns in the "Storm Path" were
Missed by the Worst of the Storms

The Reality is
Planet Earth *Has* Rain Storms
Some nastier than Others –
But it's Nothing New
And it should not Be *News*
The Reality is
Now even the Local Weathermen have Joined
The League of Extraordinary Panic-Mongers

Has anyone beside Me ever thought of Suing these People for
Terroristic- Reporting
?

Part Three

Severe Thunderstorms Headin' Our Way –
  I've actually managed
    To Live Through a Few Hundred of These
      Even been caught Out in a few of Them

Still Alive!

And yes,
  I Joyfully Confess –
I've been known to
Purposely
Walk Out Into A Storm!

It makes you feel – Alive!

It makes you feel like
  You *Are* a Part of Nature
    Like You *Belong* on This Planet

You can See God
In the Lightening Flash
You can Feel God
In the Gusting Wind
You can Touch God
In this Water of Life

You can Understand
the words
Terrible-Beauty

Part Four
(the Disharmony)

The Home of the Brave
Is Teaching It's Children
To Live in Fear

Instead of Teaching Them
To Live
  In Wonder
    And Gratitude

———————

Nobody can hurt Me
Without my Permission
Gandhi

Nothing can hurt Me
Without my Permission
Jacklin

Artificial Anxiety

One of our local television "superstations"
Strikes Again

But This One achieves Whole New Levels
Of Artificial Anxiety:

The dialogue on the show suddenly Looses All Volume –
Replaced by the Ever-Annoying
"Emergency" Beeping

Within Seconds
(about 15 of them)
A Message starts its Stately March across the screen
Bold Letters, Blocked in Red
"TORNADO WATCH"

Followed by *these* Stunning Words:
"There are No Storms
Anywhere
In this station's Viewing Area
BUT –
There Are Thunder Storms
North of our Viewing Area
(about 200 miles north by the little map…)
That COULD develop Conditions
That MAY lead to the development of Tornados in THAT Area."

"Stay Tuned to this Channel for Updates on This
Weather Event"

Perhaps we could get an update on conditions in China –
I actually have shirt-tail relatives *There*
And there are friends in California
Family in DC
And Northern Illinois
Florida
Then there's Ireland and Poland

There's Also the Possibility
Just an off-chance
That I wanted to *Watch* that Show

As sound returns just in time for the Commercials
I realize that I now have
No Clue what's going on in this Show –

I change channels

———————

Sky-Jellies

The Sky is a swift rolling tapestry of
Storm Clouds
Dark Charcoal, White, Five more Grays, Blue
And suddenly the Sky is dotted by small
Almost Black Clouds

A New Creature
A New Genus
Or perchance some mutant strain –

Sky-Jellies by the Dozens

```
               Dark Domed
            Bodies With Thick
            Depending Tentacles
          Curled into tight spirals
          W    f    p    u       a    i
          a    o    e    p       n    s
          I    r    r    o       d
          t         h    n            h
          I    s    a            C    a
          n    o    p    P       e    r
          g    m    s    I       s    d
               e         p       s
          p         t    e       n
          e    U    h    r       a    o
          r    n    e            s
          h    w    y    C   .        j
          a    a         u            u
          p    r    F    b   S        d
          s    y    e    s   c        g
                    a            a    e
               B    s            l    .
               i    t            e    .
               r                      .
               d
               ;
```

The Fear-Mongers would have me
Take Shelter
Now
But I will not miss these New Creatures of the Sky

I stand mesmerized beneath these
Wonders
(watching for small aircraft)

Now the Storm Clouds have Passed
(rainless)
The Fear Mongers say to *"Stay Alert"*

I smile
As I watch the Sky
Searching for more Sky-Jellies
(watching for small aircraft)

––––––––––––––

Anti-Bacterial Warfare

Scientific Fact:
There are Ten Times as Many
Bacteria
Living On and Living In
The Human Body
Than there are *Human Cells* in our Body

Ten to One

And That's just One Human Body
That does Not include
The Earth we Walk On
The Air we Breath
The Water we Drink

And you
Want
Anti-Bacterial Warfare –

Look Around
We Can't Win!

We're Outnumbered Ten to One
Before we take a single Step!
And the Fact is – if we Kill them All
We Die

These strange little critters
ARE
Our Friends

They help process our Food
They help fight off the "Bad Germs"
They help keep the World
The Way
It's Supposed to Be

––––––––––––––

<u>Land of War</u>

I'm watching *The Weather Channel*
They're showing a Picture:
Beautiful Blue Sky
Clean White Clouds –
The picture was sent in by one of their
"Weather Warriors"

What the hell *IS* a *"Weather Warrior"*?

Do they Single-Handedly
Beat Hurricanes back into Tropical Storms?
Do they Twist Tornados
Back into little Dust Devils?

The Weather Channel –
¿They have an Army now?

Welcome to *America – Land of War*
the War on Poverty
the War on Illiteracy
the War on Drugs
the War on Crime
the War on Cancer
the War on …

and On and On and On

Once we Encouraged Literacy
Once we only Fought Cancer
Once we only tried to Reduce the Crime Rate
But we have Escalated
Now it is full-fledged *War*
Now it is Total Annihilation
No longer will we Accept
Surrender or Peace Treaties
Now we Must Destroy All

Weather Warriors Forever!

––––––––––––––––––––

<u>Twenty-First Century American Mother</u>

Johnny! What are you Doing!?!
You Can't go out like That!

Put on your Boots and your Knee Pads
Put that Helmut on your Head this instant!
And don't forget your Wrist Guards
And Elbow Pads!

That's Better!

Now take the Bag to the Garbage Can –
But make sure you look Both Ways
Before you cross the Driveway!

Momma will watch you from the Window
And when you get back
We'll get you all washed up Nice and Clean again!

————————————

<u>Milk and Cookies</u>

What the Hell is Wrong with Us?

First We tell folks they
Shouldn't Have a Donut –
Then We try to Outlaw
Making Donuts!

Now We invade the American Home with
More *Terroristic Commercials* Declaring:
"It isn't Just Milk and Cookies –
It's Diabetes
It's Obesity and Heart Disease
It's Cancer
It's a Stroke"

It's Fucking Milk and Cookies!
It's an American Tradition!
A World Tradition!

Beyond the Fond Memories of Happy Sharing
Does anyone Remember that
Our *Species*
Has a "Sweet-Tooth" –
That virtually Every Mammal on this Planet
Has a "Sweet-Tooth"?

And Occasionally Indulging that
Craving
Is one of Life's
Sweeter Moments

One of the Oldest Foods ever found in an archeological dig was
A Pound Cake!

Can Someone *Please* give The Public –
(The *Majority* of the World)
Some Kind of Credit for
Being Able To *Think for Themselves*

Could we Please Consider the Possibility
That it *IS* Just Milk and Cookies
That it is a Treat
Given once or twice a Week –
Not a Dozen Cookies washed down by a Gallon of Milk
Twelve Times a Day!

And could We
Please
Stop Scaring our Children
Into believing that if they *Ever* eat
One Cookie
They're going to get Cancer and Die
¿
Please
?

_____

Profound Universal Truth #79

*Whether or not they Gots Toofers –
Most All God's Children
Gots
a Sweet-Toof*

_____

As Seen on the Paper Wrapper of a Future Hamburger

WARNING: *Consumption of this sandwich*
Will Not Prevent HIV or other sexually transmitted diseases

Nor will it Prevent or Lower the Risk of Heart Disease,
OCD, High Blood Pressure, or Clinical Depression

It is Not Intended to Treat Arthritis, Allergies,
Or
Any Other Disease!

It's a Fucking HAMBURGER – YOU EAT IT*

*****NOTE:*** *Hamburger should Not be Inserted into Nostrils,*
Ears, or Any Orifice Other than the Mouth

———————————

Has America ACTUALLY become THIS STUPID?

———————————

Lets talk about those little words at the bottom of TV commercials:
Car commercial: I'm watching a car drive down the road. It is driving in one lane
(it's *own* lane) and appears to be driving at a speed appropriate to the surroundings.

At the bottom of the screen appear these words:
"Closed Course. Professional Driver. Do Not Attempt."
?
Shit! I thought you was tryin' to sell me a car I could drive on the Road –
I didn't Know that it was some kind of Trick Car –
it *Looked* like a Real car you could drive on Real Roads…

———————————

Addendum: Almost two years later, Deirdre and I caught a car ad which proclaimed
Their Cars were "Designed for Real Roads" – *It's a thought –*

———————————

82

The HHMI Blues

Double-Parked?
What are you talking about?

I've got to get to my Doctor Now!
There were 17 new drugs on TV
Just this week
And I've got to Ask him about All of them
(They *said* I had to ask him!)
Don't you have any Compassion?
Any sense of Humanity?

My God, I've got COPD, OCD, ADHD, RLS,
ED, STD, HIV, HBP, ACS,
CRS, HDTV, NSA, and
FB Eye!

And I've got to get to my Pharmacist to discuss Drug Interactions –
You know Doctors never know about That…

And now you're making me Late!
I was supposed to take these three pills
Four and a Half Minutes Ago!

My God, you're one of Them!

You're trying to Kill Me!

———————

Treat a man as he is and he will remain as he is.
Treat a man as he can and should be
and he will become as he can and should be.
Goethe

Jacklin's Corollary: Treat someone as a Moron long enough, and
They Will Become a Moron.

Land of the Free

The *Land of the Free* has
Become
Bound to and by
Ubiquitous-Authority

It is as if We have Given-Up our Right to Think
As if We have Signed-in-Blood some
Binding Document
Which *Forbids* us to Think for Ourselves
Which Requires We Seek only
Approved Experts
For the Smallest Choices in
Our Lives

We are no longer Free
To Decide for Ourselves or
To Act on our own

The Land of the Free
No Longer Desires
The Individual
To Be
Independent

American-Independence
Has been replaced by *Learned-Helplessness*
The *Home of the Brave*
Now lives in *Constant-Fear*
Fear of Terrorists
Fear of AIDS

Fear of Diseases – Unheard of –
Until the Commercial that just ended
Fear of the Food we Eat
Food which has Fed Us for Millennia!

Fear of Living –

84

DRUG TEST

Drug-Testing
Falls into the Same Category as
Paparazzi –

It's No One Else's Business!

I was Trained as a Drug Rehab Councilor –
THESE are Facts:
It's NOT "Drugs **and** Alcohol"
Alcohol **IS** a Drug
Alcohol is the **Number One**
Used and
Ab-used
Drug
On This Planet!

I am soon to be Scheduled for Yet Another
Drug (USE) Test

I have never Failed these Tests
Yet, I *AM* a Drug User
I Use
My Drugs
On a Daily Basis
Yet
THESE Drugs Are Accepted –
And have Approval
Approaching (until recently) an
Almost Loving Embrace

Fact: Not ALL
Drugs
are
the Same

Fact: Not ALL
Drug Users
are Ab-users

Fact: Not ALL
Drug Users
Use Drugs
At Work

I've even heard of a Company
Which would
Very Soon
Test their Employees
For
Tobacco Use
On *Non-Working* Hours!

(I'm sorry, Mr. Gates, but on *This** You are Wrong!)

NO ONE
NO ONE
NO ONE
At Any Time
Any Where
Under Any Circumstances
HAS the Right
To
In Any Way
Control or Restrict
The LIFE of Another

.

NO ONE
Has the Right to Impose Themselves into the LIFE of
ANOTHER

.

The *Artist*
Does Not Perform
Twenty-Four Hours per Day

They Too
are People –
It is ONLY
a Different Job
than Ours

Even the Most
Dedicated
Absorbed
Obsessed Performer
Has Some Part of their Life
which Should be Considered as Private

(On *This***, Mr. Heinlein is most Correct!)

NO ONE
Deserves to have their LIFE
Invaded
Infringed
or Impeded by ANOTHER.

Let the Smokers
Smoke
Be It Tobacco or Hashish
Let the Drinkers
Drink
Be It Beer or Absinth

If I have Wine with dinner Seven Nights a Week…
Ain't Nobody's Business
But My Own!

Let Each Find
Their *Own* Path through Life –
Each Seeks Happiness
In Their Own Way –
Let Each BE

If we can LEARN this *Simple Truth*
If we can ALLOW
Others to Walk Their Path
Unhindered
Than Perhaps
We can Learn to ALLOW
OurSelf
To Walk Our Own Path
Unconcerned

***Ain't Nobody's Business
But My Own!***

––––––––––

* Bill Gates is involved in an effort to stop tobacco use WORLDWIDE.
Fact: A few decades ago, France led the world in per capita cigarette consumption. At the same time, they had the lowest incidence of lung cancer amongst the developed nations of the world.

** Robert A. Heinlein, proposed in several of his stories, a future in which all paparazzi – including "legitimate" newsmen – were required By Law to instantly grant privacy to any celebrity (to *any* person) if that person requested it.

Fact: Ain't Nobody's Business –
But My Own!

––––––––––

<u>Profound Universal Truth #516</u>

*Drugs are for those who can't handle
Reality*

———————————

<u>Profound Universal Truth #517</u>

*Reality is for those who can't handle
Drugs*

———————————

<u>Profound Universal Truth #518</u>

*To USE Drugs
Or
To USE Reality –*

Each is Truth.

*Neither is Right
And
Neither is Wrong*

———————————

The Law of Anarchy

Anarchists Arise!

We Must
Somehow Stop this Madness!

We Must
Abolish All Laws which Restrict
Total Freedom!

If Man needs a "Law" – Let it Be This:

*"No One Shall
At Any Time
INTERFERE
With the LIFE of ANOTHER
nor
At Any Time
ATTEMPT to Control the Actions of, or
by Any Means
Impose THEIR Will upon,
ANOTHER
except Where such action is
Mutually and Contractually
Agreed Upon
For
A Specified Period of Time
To perform Specified Duties
or Complete Specified Tasks"*

i.e. AT WORK!

———————

Part two – getting to know myself

During my college days I wrote frequently, but "life" kind of got in the way of Living and I only wrote on the rare inspired days; until my father passed away. That event seemed to break open a flood of memories and the need to express them. It also returned me to my Great Quest.

The following are excerpts from a very long and personal opus written in the week after his death. They are included now only to share my Starting Point.

Call From My Sister

I play the message – It's tearing her up
(Be Happy – the Son-of-a-Bitch is Gone!)

I suppose I should feel sorrow
But mostly I feel Nothing
He has been Gone from My Life for Many Years

It just doesn't Feel like there is any Great Loss

_____

The Day

Visitation: That most aptly named event
Reunions – Tempered by Time
Apologies for the Circumstances
Promises for the Future

The Internment: Front Row Center
It feels very Strange and Surreal
Like suddenly being made the Lead in a Play
But no one has given me a Script

Afterwards: Good Food, Good Company
And I'll not complain of another *Bailey's*
Late supper – Tired
I think of writing
And go to bed

_____

Scattered Memories and Emotional Emptiness

I do not regret Hating him – It Is What It Is
He spent many years behind a Wall of Emotional Solitude
And when he came Out
It was only to share his Disappointment in Me

90

90

earliest memory:

<u>The Garden Next Door</u>

It was like crossing some Invisible Threshold
A Magick Portal to Another World – *Mr. Spinello's Garden*

Great Spires of Colors and Greens
And Carpets of Soft Petals all 'round
Red Brick Walks in Patterns and Circles
All tended by Big Fat Bumble Bees and Giant Hornets
And Ants
And Beetles
And Humming Birds
Under a Great Shining Dome of Blue and White

And I wanted to Stay Forever!

I can't remember exactly –
I was only four or five
But I have an "Impression-of-a-Memory"
Something like "Flowers are for girls"

But it was all So Beautiful!
And I don't remember a Mrs. Spinello

---

age six or seven:

<u>The Family Cry</u>

Some kind of an argument between Mom and Dad –
And my sisters were somehow "involved"

As the event reached a cathartic end –
Tears and Hugs and "I'm Sorry's" all 'round
Even from my father

I had been standing on the outside
Surrounded by – Sliced by these Emotions
Not Understanding
But I start to cry
"I'm sorry Too"

Maybe I was his "last straw" –
"What the Hell are *you* sorry for?!"
"You're not even Part of this!"

And Boy, I *Felt* It
Not Part of Anything

---

teenager:

<u>Memory-Fragment / Realization</u>

I remember going with to Marilyn & Bill's partly built new home
He told me to do something or get something for him
And I did it Wrong

He instantly let me know It was Wrong
I was Wrong – I was Worthless
Bill came to the rescue, yelling back
"How do you expect him to Know what to Do
When you Never Taught him Anything?"

Now I Know he Did Teach Me –

"You're not Good Enough"
"You'll Never be Good Enough"
"You Can't make a living as an Artist – and If you Could
It just wouldn't be *Right*"
And *Those* Lessons I Learned

Too Well

―――――――

grown-up:

<u>Birthday Party</u>

I have twenty-plus people Praising my Cooking
Kudos from Strangers

And the Guest of Honor
True Chef in all but Paper, and close to That
Pays me Homage

And I think, "These people are nuts"
I'm translating Sautéed into Grilled
By a Factor of Five
And I'm "winging-it" on stuff I've never made Before
In a Kitchen too small for a Roach

And as soon as it was Done
I had a list of "Ten Things to Make It Better"

Yes, I have Leaned my Lessons Well

―――――――

the epiphany: I still have no Tears for my father. But I now have something I've
never had before – a small place in my Heart for Him. He
Truly was one of the Great
Negative-Teachers

―――――――――――――

<u>Thoughts on Self-Image</u>

We must – *Each of Us* – Awaken
We must *Each*
Recognize our Worth, our Potential

We must Learn to Love
To Truly, Deeply, Utterly
Love
OURSELVES

We stand before our Mirrors
Seeing *Not* Reality
But only the Years of Lies

Believing the Voices of Old
Our Parents
Our Teachers
Our Leaders
Our Clergy
Telling us We are not Good Enough
Smart Enough
That We are not Worthy

But that kind of Perfection is Death
That Perfection is the End of Growth

And We are not meant to be Angels –
The Angels pretty much Have that Covered

Yet We Are
Children of God
Each of Us a Beloved Child of God

To make a mistake – in Any way
Is but Opportunity to Learn
To Grow

And with all our Mistakes
Our Greed's and Lust's
Our Anthems of Right and Wrong
With all of Our Divine-Imperfections
We Are
Always Good Enough
Always Worthy
We Are Always Lovable

We Are

————————

<u>Gratitude</u>

I am Grateful for All my
Incredible Fuck-Ups
Stupid Choices
and
For the Cruel and Mean things I have Done

I am Grateful for
My Lying
Thieving
Cheating
For playing on others' emotions
For playing *with* others' emotions
For Using others

I am Grateful for my outbursts of Emotional-Psychosis
and
For my great bouts of Depression
Even when they seemed Never-Ending

I Thank You All

I Thank You Each for your Experience
And for your Lessons – your True Gifts to me

For without Lies
I would not have learned the Value of Truth

Without Cheating
I would not have learned the True Joy of Winning

Without Meanness
I would not have learned the Wonder of True Caring
the Beauty of Tenderness

Without Each and Every One of You
and Dozens More –
Without You All, I would not Be
NOW
Who I Am
What I Am
Where I Am

I Thank You!

––––––––––

Being Myself

Devil Saint Savior
Fool

Deluded Deranged Depraved

Psycho
Lost Soul

All of that …And More
All and None

I Am to Each
Whatever
They Believe I Am

But I *Am*
What *I* Am!

And More…

———————

Average Parent

What to Do…What to Do
I Write
I Sculpt

I can't pick One over the Other
They are Both my Children

Each Unique and Each Loved Equally

I guess some days
I Prefer to Write
Some days
I Prefer to Sculpt

Some days
I think the DVD
Is God's Greatest Gift to Humanity

I guess that makes me
An Average Parent

———————

Self-Discovery Snapshot

I always say –
If you can't Amaze 'Em
Amuse 'Em!

And I am Discovering
That
Seems to Be my
Mission-In-Life –
The Essence of my Life

It's like "the Effect" I Am

I'm having this sudden Image –
A kind of Montage of my Life
All these moments
Overlapping
Forming a Multi-Dimensional Snapshot

I can See there is a Pattern
A Motif of Actions
Works of
Art
Things that end up either
Amazing someone
Or Amusing them

The Best Stuff does Both!

I Like it!
I Think I'll Keep Me!

———————

Profound Universal Truth #213

Spontaneous Ear-Hair Growth
Is God's Way
Of Keeping the Ego in check

—————————————

Be Not Proud and Boastful
— But Humility is a Bunch o' Hooey —

Thou Art God Incarnate!

The Transcendence of Wine

It is the Perfect Balance of
God and Man
It is the Divinity of the Flesh
It is the Delicate Balance of
Man and God

Too much
And the Universe can collapse into Blackness
But there is a Point
Which
Transcends mere Drunkenness

A Point at which One
Achieves
Startling Clarity
and
Blissful Acceptance
A *Knowing* that

All Is As It Should Be!

A *Knowing* that
It Could Be
No Other Way
It is Life
Unfolding

This is Wine's *Raison D'Etre*

Another Godling –
Stretching its Wings
Effortlessly
Being

———

<u>Song for Bacchus</u>

A Wine-High Night!
What a
  Delight
    !

'Sposed to be
        a-Typin'
      But
I'm a-Writin'
        'Stead

The Wine
  FREES
My Spirit
    Goes To My Head –
Make's me ThinkS my Name
        'S   Fred
          But Poems comes
    Outs M'Han's – so's
maybe
  Just calls me
    Stan...

(Luv Ya, Bacchy – Bye-Bye!)

———————————

<u>Allowing My Self</u>

God, I Love This!
Letting my Self write *Through* myself –

It's like someone has a Magic Camera:
  They take a movie of me –
    Writing
      In the Future

        Close up of the Hands upon the Paper
    The Pen Dancing and Flying
As it dots the "i"s

Then they show me the movie –
  And I *Know* it's Me
    I Feel the Pen in Hand
      I Taste the Cigarette –
      I Flick the Ashes!
      I *Know* it's Me

      And the Whole Time I'm watching
  This Movie
There's a part of me Thinking:

Ooh! I wonder What he's going to write Next!

When I catch *That* moment, I Know –
  The World is Perfect
    And Everything is Good

Everything is God

———————

The Lonesome God Blues

Feeling very *Alone* in All of This right Now

I Know – I Know
We Are Never Alone
All Is One
I Know!
Been There; Felt That
I DO Understand –
I've just got
A Bad Case of the Lonesome God Blues
I want Someone to Talk to –
Someone *Else* Who Understands
This *Stuff* –

These Words that Pour out of my Pen!
Sometimes it Feels like They have
a Mind of Their Own
And They Want Out Now!
It's not a Desperation –
But there Does seem to Be an
Urgency

There are days I'm totally Amazed
I did Anything besides Write

But it's Not Me Doing the Writing!

OK, I *Know* it *Is* Me
But not the Everyday Me
Not the Shopper
Dish Washer
Cook
Kind of Me
I Understand
It is My *Inner Self*
The Godhead
The Christ-Consciousness
The Whole-I-Spirit
Speaking *Through Me*

And even though the Words come Through Me –
Sometimes
The Results Feel Very
¿Not-Me?

Sometimes I Have to Really *Read* It
To Know what I Just Wrote!
Other times it's like I *Know* what I Just Wrote
I mean KNOW IT
Know It as Absolute Truth
I can completely understand
What I just wrote –

But I Can't *Feel* It
It's not Really Mine yet!

I want Someone to Talk to –
Someone Who Understands This Stuff
Someone Who Understands
The Lonesome God Blues

BLOSSOM

There is a Frustration
That comes With the Learning
A Frustration of Wanting to Share
THIS – Which has No Words

Life-Changing Concepts
Are like small buds upon the branches of a tree
I Feel the Concepts – Waiting – Growing
Starting to Blossom
To BECOME
That which is Beyond Words

The Meanings can be *Felt*
But cannot be Translated
– I have No Words –

Words can only Hint
Paint Vague Images
Which fade like Morning Mist

There is a Frustration –
I cannot *Talk* about It
Even to Myself

<u>Learning to Talk with Myself</u>

I am Learning to Talk with Myself
Questions come easily enough
Sometimes Unbidden

But the Answers –

Learning to Listen
Without *Expectation*
To Listen without *Fear*

Learning to *Feel* the Response of
Both *self* and *Self*
As this New Form of Dialogue
Emerges

This is somehow Different than Before
It is Almost
As if my *Self*
Could At Last
Stand
and
Stretch

It is Good!

__Human-Ness__

Well, I just did it Again –
And in Reality, it doesn't even Matter
What IT is –
It could be the ever popular
Walk into a room to Get something
And you Can't Remember What…
Only the Entire World Does That

So now it's Choice Time – Or not such a Choice-Time

First Reaction is –
"You Fucking Idiot!"
"You're about Useless!"
"Here's Proof – a Fifth-Grader IS Smarter"
But I actually Stop myself
And ask *Why* –

Why am I beating myself up?
All I did was commit another act of
Unadulterated Human-ness
And I don't even *have* to Judge it –

It Was
And
I AM
And That's That
!

————

Forgiving

I Understood – the Basics –
        The Theoretical Approach
        But putting Theory into Practice –
Not So Much

I've Done it Before
  But always with some Reluctance
    Some Hesitation
      Like trying to Hold your Mouth
      Just So
        To Pronounce some Foreign Word

      But This was Different
      This had an Ease about it
    Some indescribable
    Gracefulness –
      Like a Magical Dance
        Beneath a Full Moon
         A Rightness to it –
      To Truly Forgive
      Perhaps for the Very First Time

  This had a natural
Comfortableness
In both the Receiving and the Giving

Forgiving Myself
  This had a
    Natural Balance

———————

<u>It Ain't Easy</u>

I think Too Many of the
Contemporary Teachers
Have a habit of Presenting this New Way of Living as
Easy

And overall I think this
"Hurts the Cause"
It allows people to get Discouraged
It makes for Easy Quitting

We Want the Whole World to Wake Up
To start Living Consciously
To start Consciously Allowing

Yes – the *Living Part* of this New Way
IS
Easy
But few talk about how Hard it can Be
Getting There

Most of Us were Taught Wrong
Most of Us have Decades of
Negative Programming
Conflicting Beliefs
Poor Self Esteem
Poor Self Image
Cultural Guilt
Religious Guilt

Most of Us have Co-Workers
Friends
Parents
Siblings
Spouses
Who do Not Understand

And Most of Us have a Major Case of
Self Doubt

It can be Hard to Keep Going
Keep working on this
Self Awareness
It can be Tiring
To *Start*
Again and Again and Again

Yet Ever Must We Try
For there *Really* seems to Be
No Other
Sane Approach to Living

The *Reality* of Our World is Not So Easy
To Understand –
That Time IS an Illusion
AND Real
At the Same Time
That We Really are *Creating* the World
As We Look Upon It
That there Really Is No
One World
Which All Can Perceive and Agree Upon
The *Reality* of Our World is Not So Easy to Understand

But the *Living-In* Our World Can be Learned
The *Utter Simplicity* of The Law of Attraction
Can be Understood

If not the *Why* of It – At Least *the Way of It*

And the Learning Is Not Hard
The Lessons are Not Hard to Understand
Intellectually

But it Does Take
Practice and Persistence and Patience
We can't just Read the Lessons and Learn
We Must Live the Lessons

And It Ain't Easy

———————

Living the Lessons

(for Tony)

I ran into one of my "Fans" today
At the Grocery Store –
First I have to say
As Artist, I've had Fans before
As Poet, I've had Fans also
But that was somehow Different –

They only Read my Words
They were Fans of Paper
They were mostly Friends
Now, I'm Reading in Public
Mostly to Strangers
And the *Topic* is Different –
These are now Fans of the *Message*
As well as my Words

I am Humbled, Awed, Amazed
That I am Touching the Spirits of Others –
To Touch the Spirit of Self
or Other is
Always a Wonder and a Blessing for All

But I suddenly have Fans again – a New Kind of Fan
(I Am a New Kind of Me)

So, here I am in the *Kroger Store*
Actually, the Reality is that I am Not –
In the *Kroger Store*
Instead of Now Here
I am Nowhere

I have let my Mind wander off again –
Still bemused at what *Kroger* Didn't Have
And Considering Alternatives of Procurement
Thinking about Chores and Choices that Wait for Me at Home
I am Even Thinking about "the Book"
Thinking about the Book –

But Not *Living the Lessons!*

*The Messiah's Handbook** is Absolutely Right –
"You Teach Best what You Most Need to Learn"
Or as *someone* has said, on *more* than *one occasion,*
We Need to Do the Homework

OK – so I'm Not-Here – with a man standing in front of me
I recognize him, but I cannot Place him
In Time or Space
When he tells me of the circumstances
I have vague memories of –
No Pita Pockets!
What kind of *Kroger* is this?
And I Really, Really DO have to Cut the Lawn Tonight
– Hack through the Jungle!

I *Do* Remember you –
Need to work on the Book
And Call Guin tomorrow
And Marilyn
And Write that Note to Aunt Edna

There *Is* some part of me
That's Becoming Aware that I'm Not Really *Here*
And I seem to be Not-Arriving Soon
Yeah – Need to *DO* the Homework
Need to *Live the Lessons*
and
Need to Apologize to Tony when I see him Next

———————————

*As presented by Richard Bach in ***Illusions***

Epitaph to a Chance Encounter

It was a Not So Subtle Reminder
I've been kinda *No-where* for Several Days now

The Simplicity of Awareness Awaits Us All
Yet We return to Old Habits again and again

Last Night my Higher Self Channeled-On-In
And I was *Teaching* this Very Lesson

Today I Learn It
Again

———————————

Judgment

Working at *Planet-Porno**
In the Beginning
It was All Judgment

It was Easy – just Pre-Judge Each Person
Perverts and
Deviants
Sex Addicts and
Lost Souls

But, I Have Learned – They are Doctors,
Lawyers,
Judges,
Librarians;
They Change Tires,
and Build Houses;
They have Children
and Pets –
Birds, Dogs, Cats, Fish, even Spiders and Snakes

They are from Here – and Canada
New Zealand
and Mexico
China
and England

Some read the Classics
Some read the Newspaper
Some read Science Fiction
Some read Deepak Chopra

I Have Learned – They Are You
And They Are Me

---

*I was once employed as a sales clerk at an Adult Book Store/Theater – this accounts for the reference to "Planet Porno" (not the real name).

Look upon your Neighbor
As you would have Him
Look upon You

Leading Horses

I've often wondered if Just Possibly
The Great Teachers
Ever Just
LOST IT
!

Jesus *Did* have that one Morning at the Temple
And there *Was* that Zen Master who Hacked Off his Student's Arm!
(but That actually worked out well…)

But Over All – the "Bigger-Hammer Technique" just Doesn't Work
It Tends to Break Bones
And Stress Relationships

But I Do get Saddened and Frustrated
To Watch – Anyone – Friend, Brother, Stranger
Start on the Path
Start to Understand
Start even to See Results
And then They Stop…

And as I Thank my Frustration and Sadness
Several Lessons come to my mind –

We Can Not DO For Another
We Must Each Walk Our Own Path
You Can Lead a Horse to Water…
Everything Is As It Should Be

ALLOW ALL!

———————

Profound Universal Truth #12

*As the Self is Ready
So shall It Learn*

———————

<u>Earthlings</u>

I was raised by a *Proud Polack*
A man who *Knew*
There were None-Better than the Poles
And None-Worse than
The Russians
The Italians
The Romanians
And the Jews
And don't forget the Gypsies!

It made no difference that he had Never set foot in Poland
That he was Born in America
He *Was Polish!*

And even in my Youth
And Worldly Innocence
I Knew he was so full of Pure Crap
I just couldn't stand it...

For years I've tried to Explain to people
I don't *Think* of Myself As
Democrat or Republican or Libertarian
As An American
Or Even as White or Black or Red

I don't Think of Anyone Else
As Russian
Or Chinese
Or even Polish
I've tried to Explain –
All People
Are Just People

Different Languages
Different Costumes
Different Customs
These are Differences
That Mean
Nothing

No more than whether someone lives
On the East side of town or the West

These Things
Are Circumstance Only
They Do Not Change
What we Are
They Do Not Change
How we Are

They Do Not Change
The Need for Food and Water
Shelter
They Do Not Change
The Need for Companionship
The Need for Love
Sharing

They Do Not Change
The Desire for Happiness
The Desire for a Good Life
The Desire to Live
In Peace and Safety
With people we Choose

Circumstances Cannot Define Us
Cannot Make Us
Less than Human
Or even More than Human

Circumstances Do Not Change
The Fact that We are All

Earthlings

———————

My Worst-Best Day Ever

Part One: I Quit!
Major Irwin Justin Cant, Reporting for Duty!
To those who know him well –
I. Just Cant *or* I. Cant

That's what it Feels Like –
I could just Stop Dead in my tracks
Curl up in a Ball
And Die

Or at least Plunge Willing into Vegetative-Depression
Visit with this Old Friend
For an Indefinite Period of Time
But *Definitely* something Lengthy

Sure! Be a Living Example!
Demonstrate the Truth of These Words
The Power of These Words

But My Truth is Shaken
My Power is Wounded
I have Demonstrated Only Failure –

I Just Can't Try Anymore!
I have Waited in Faith
But Now I am Empty of Faith
Empty of Waiting
I have No Power

I have Guarded against the Black Magicians
Yet They have Won
I now have No Strength to Ward Off Their Lies
I Just Can't Do It Anymore –
I Just Don't Care Anymore

I have Envisioned Myself
Successful
Respected
Artist / Writer
I have *Seen* These Things
I have *Felt* These Things *As Real!*

Now, All are Shadows in the Darkness

I have Done My Best and I am Lost
I am Empty of All Knowing
All Faith
All Hope
All Passion for Life Itself

Unending Abundance and Total Freedom
Taunt Me!
Standing Just There – Out of Reach
I Understand Now those Words –
"Why Hast Thou Forsaken Me?"

Part Two: Lost and Overwhelmed by Doubt
Caught up in this Sudden Attack
This Unexpected Battle against These Old Emotions
Old Feelings
Old Thoughts
They Fight Again to Fill My Life
To *Be* My Life

And Now I Am Beaten
And I Write my Last Words
Yet even As I Surrender Totally
Before the Ink which Forms These Words has Dried
I Feel Their Grip of Death
Loosening –
I Feel Their Power Dimming
Exhausted and Drained
Yet I *Feel* Again!
From the Emptiness that Consumed Me
I *Feel* Again
My Faith Reawakening

I *Feel* Again
The Power Within Me Stir
Quietly, I Hear These Truths again
And Know, They will Out

Exhausted and Drained – *Yet I Am*

And I Know Now that I Have No Other Path
And though I May Need Battle Again
These Old Foes –
I Know Again
I Am

———

It Is So Easy

It's All so Easy
It Really Is
It's Just a matter of
Deciding –
Choosing This Life
Over the Old Way

It Is Literally a Thought Away

I've Done It! I Know It Works
But It is So Easy
To Fall back to Old Ways
Old Habits
It is So Easy
To Think: *At Last I've Got It*
And the very Next Instant –
Shall I just say "Not Got It"

I get headed in the Right Direction
I even Stay On-Course for several days – Longer
Then I run into one of my Personal Land Mines
The Lingering Legacy of
Pre-Conscious Thought Patterns

BOOM!

All New Habits and Better Thoughts Blown Away

And since *Something* Has to Fill the Void –
Re-enter the Old Ways
Always Waiting in the Wings

It Is So Easy
To Feel like *A Ping-Pong Ball*
In China

———

<u>Getting It</u>

Eventually
I Might *Get* This

I Get-It over Here
And I don't Get-It over There
So That means
I Really *Don't* Get-It

But I'm Starting to Get-It
And I'm getting Lots Quicker in Recognizing When
I Don't Got-It

That's a Good Step!

And I Think that
Thinking
Gets in the Way of Getting-It
Gets in the Way
of *Letting-It*

That Is the Goal – isn't it?

We keep working at it - Practicing
Until we Finally
Understand
That it's Not *About* Understanding

It's about *Letting* our *Total Self*
Be
ItSelf

The Right Path

Sometimes I feel so *Frustrated* –
It's like Half a Century!
(OK – 47 years, but who's counting?)
I keep Learning
And I keep Forgetting

Or should I say: I have as Yet been unsuccessful in my efforts
To internalize my lessons in a manor
which would make them
More readily Available for Effective Daily Use

Or, more succinctly stated as:
AAAAAAAAAARRRRRRRGGGGGGGGG!!!

And I have to Laugh at myself
And I have to Forgive myself
As I Remember an Old Lesson:

You Get What You Want
When You Get what you Got!

And Truly, I have Loved my Path
(most of it anyway – still working on the rest)
Even that for which I haven't any great Fondness
I could not easily wish to change
For it – *every part* – has brought me *Here*

I just need to remember –
On those Days
When I just want to
StartAllOverItWouldJustBeEasierPlease!

I need to remember –

My Path
IS
The Right Path for Me

My Gifts

Writer: I Understand Now
That My Gift to the World Is
My Perspective
My Expression of Life

I Understand Now
That My Words
Can Shine a Light of New Understanding
Can Add-Unto the World
New-Words of Truth
Timeless Truth
Ageless Truth
Truth which has Always Been
Spoken now only by *Another* Voice
Spoken now from a different Place in Time

I Know Now
That these New-Words of Truth
Can Help Others
In Their Journeys
That these New-Words
Can Help Others *Hear*
the Calling of Their Own Heart
That these New-Words of Understanding
Will Help Lift the World

Sculptor: I Understand Now
That My Gift to the World Is
My Perspective
My Expression of Life

Taking the Lost and the Discarded and the Broken
Things of Others
And Giving New Life – New Form
That Others may
See My Vision
Hold My Vision
Touch and Turn it in their Hands
Seeing
Both *the Old* and *the New*

Seeing *Both*

In an Old Way
And
In a New Way

I Understand Now
These are the Gifts of My Heart
And that the Abundance of the Universe
Is Mine
That I may Create
Freely
That I may Give
Joyously

I Thank God for These Gifts
That I May Share
With the World

ALIVE

I Feel
Miracles inside me –
Changes
Events
Occurrences
Things Which Are At the Very Edge of Belief

Yet I Know
T'is Naught of Magick Born

No Magick
White
or
Black
Could ever approach *This*

For This is
The Law
Alive
Within Me!

Chapter Four

Doing The Homework

"Between stimulus and response, man has the freedom to choose."
Viktor Frankl

Preludes

The Seeking

Hurry, Hurry!
Become the Master
Of Your Own Fate!

Become As a God
Amongst the Common Man!

Change Your Entire Life
In Just 30 Days!

We *Hear* the Voices Urging Us
Like Barkers at a Carnival

We *Hear* the Voices –
Because We have been Too Well Conditioned
To Seek Ever
In the World about Us

For Reasons
For Answers
For Solutions
For Teachers
And They may All Help

But If They
Be
True Answers
True Solutions
True Teachers

They can only Point
Back to Our Own Self

They can *Do* No More than
Stand upon the Shore, Encouraging
As We Alone
Step Boldly into the Great Ocean of Wonder
That Is Our Own True Self

– Our Totality –

But Before We can Truly Explore
These Unending Depths
We Must Accept that We *Are* the Creators of Our Own Life
And for Too Many of Us
It is Easier to
To Seek Ever Outside OurSelf

Seeking the ONE Guru
Who will Tell Us that it *Really Was*
Bad Luck
An Accident
Someone *Else's* Fault
Even *Knowing* It Would All Be Lies

Seeking Ever for the ONE System
In Which
No Work of *Any* Kind is Required to Produce *Change*
Knowing This Too Is A Lie

Perhaps there *is* some Quirk of Human Nature
Which makes us Afraid of Power
But I think it More Likely
Just Bad Training
and
Wrong Training

Like the Irony of being Called *Human Beings*
And being Taught
That our Only Value lies in
Human Doings

And the Error of being Taught
That We Must
Become
When the Reality Is
We Already Are

———————————

<u>CHANGING</u>

Stop Worrying about it –
It's only Change
We are Changing All the Time
And We don't even Notice till Long Time Later – if Then!

Change is The Way of Life

We're Not gonna turn into some kind of
Weird Monster
And We're Not gonna turn into some kind of
Reluctant Saint either –

We are In Charge!

No one else Can do This *For Us*
And no one else Can do This *To Us*
Just like the Rest of Life –

We are What Happens to Us

And Remember –
Every last little bit of This
Is Already Within Us
Always Has Been
Always Will Be

All the Affirmations
Exercises
Practices
Prayers and Meditations
Etc. Etc.
Are Designed for One Thing Only –

To help Us Remember!

———————————

TEACHERS and STUDENTS

I was thinking today about the Great Teachers:
Krishna
Jesus of Nazareth
Buddha
Muhammad
G'Kar of Narn

Were They *REALLY?*
I mean "Great Teachers"

Not a Single One of Them
Ever said,
"Worship Me"
Yet we turn Them into Resin Cast Idols
And Dashboard Dolls
(I'm pretty sure there is at least one Mirror-Air-Freshener out there)

And *All* the Lessons were pretty simple and straight forward –
We Are All One
We Are United – Inseparable
Love One Another
The Evidence is Everywhere
The Truth is Within You
Go Within

So What the Hell Happened?!?!?!

I was thinking today about the Great Teachers
If They Really Were Great Teachers –
That makes *Humanity*
The Spiritual-Sweat-Hogs of the Universe!

"Ooh, ooh – Teacher!
Could you explain that AGAIN..."

Yes, Child – I will explain – AGAIN
But you must remember
*That Until you **Do** the Homework*
You won't Really
Learn –

ANYTHING

———————

<u>WHY?</u>

Why are We
So Lazy?

We Know Better –
Intellectually
We can Follow this Logic
We can Understand
How this Works

We See it in Action daily
In the Lives of those around Us
And Sometimes We will even Admit
It is going on in
Our Own Life

Yet, Still We Do Nothing
To Change Ourself
Almost as if We fear
Awakening to find a Stranger
As if We would no longer
Know Ourself

But We Do Not Know Ourself Now!

We are Told
We are Shown
Sometimes –
For a Brief Moment
We can Feel
Our True Self
We can Feel this Law
In Action
And then We let it Fade
As if it were No More than a Dream

Why?

———

<u>Doing the Homework</u>

We need to Do the Homework!

This is Not a One-Shot Deal!
One Time
And All is Well

This is Not just a Fact
To be Stored Away in some Dusty Corner of our Mind
Until Needed

This is Not like a 9 to 5 Job
Mon through Fri
We can't "leave *This* at the Office"
(and Who would *Want* To?)

And this is Not like Traditional Homework – Do it and Forget it

This is more like Live-in Kindergarten

This Is a Life-Commitment
To Joy
To Health
To Wealth
To True Peace
But first is Kindergarten

First we need to Learn the Basics

But to Truly *Learn* –
We need to *Do* the Homework:
We need to Live these Lessons

Then it *Is* like a Job
The kind you can Do
without even thinking about it…
Then We Are Free!

We need to Do the Homework!

––––––––––––––––––––

Part one – the basics

<u>We Must Believe</u>

We Cannot *Use*
What We Do Not Believe-In
We Cannot even Start to Change
Anything
About Our Life or
About Our Self
Until
We Admit To Ourself
We Are Responsible For Our Life

We Must Acknowledge To Ourself
That *The Actions* We Have Taken Freely
That *The Choices* We Have Made
Are
What have brought Us
Here
Now

We Must Accept the *Reality* of
The Law of Attraction
We Must Accept the *Reality* of
Being Gods

We Must *Know*
We Create Our Own Reality

We Cannot *Use*
What We Do Not Believe-In
We Must Believe
NOW

———

The Law of Attraction

"That which is like unto itself, is drawn."
Abraham, as channeled by Ester Hicks

"Like attracts Like"

"Like unto like doth the universe cry
What thou choose to accept thou wilt see
Skim the wide ocean, split the deep sky
Relentlessly bound on a meeting with thee"
U.S. Anderson, *Three Magic Words*

"Your Thoughts and Beliefs create Your Reality."

"This Law of Attraction is no joke, no metaphysical absurdity,
but a great live working principle of Nature, as anyone may
learn by experimenting and observing."
Steven R. Covey, *The 7 Habits of Highly Effective People*

"What you Think about, you Bring about."

The Law of Attraction is *Why*
Science Developed the
"Double Blind" Experiment
Science Knows
We Create Our Own Reality

"Thoughts Become Things."

THE LAW OF ATTRACTION
Regardless How it is Worded
Regardless What Language
Regardless Who Says It
IS
THEE
UNIVERSAL *LAW OF LIFE*

There are many attempts to Explain
Exactly How it Works –
The Electro-Magnetic Nature of Thoughts and Emotions
Matching Vibrational Frequencies, Etc

"Birds of a feather, flock together."

But the How it Works
the Why it Works
Just Doesn't Matter!
THE LAW OF ATTRACTION
Is The One and Only

Fact Of Life
This Is The Way Life Works
!

You Can't Stop It from Working
There Is No Way to Shut It Off
It Is Always Working
Whether YOU Believe in it or Not

It Is Always Working
Whether YOU Like it or Not
There is Nothing in the Universe
Which can Change It
Or Stop It
IT IS – Period

But We Have the Power
To Use It Consciously
We Have the Ability
To Use It Consciously

"Ask and ye shall Receive"

No One Tries to Deny
The Law of Gravity
No One Tries to Deny
The Existence of Electricity
Neither are fully Understood –
Yet We Accept their Daily Use and Influence as Natural

And still, as a Species
We Deny the Reality of This Law
As a Species, We Strive to Ignore This Law –
Endlessly Seeking
OTHER EXPLANATIONS

This Law – Its Existence
And How To Use It
How To Control It
For the Betterment of All
Has been Taught By
Every Avatar

Now, We have This Reality –
The Law of Attraction *IS*
Scientific Fact

And Still We Strive to
Deny
Ignore
Refuse

Refute
World Wide
There are No Schools which *Teach* This Law
Even in the Science classes
Even in the Philosophy classes
It is Rarely Mentioned

If I *Believed* in Some Heavenly Father
I would Pray
That every person upon this Earth
Every man, every woman, every child
Would Awaken in the Morning
To Find a Report Card from God
And This Report Card would include
One Subject Only –
The Law of Attraction

And Every Card would be Marked
"UNSATISFACTORY"

As a Species, We Need to Wake Up
We Need to Accept the Universe
As It Is
We Need to Accept Ourselves
As We Are

We Must Learn to
Use
The Law of Attraction

Profound Universal Truth #17

The Law is Everything.

<u>BECAUSE</u>

There actually Is
True Logic in This most Basic of Laws
– The Law of Attraction –

But it is not a Logic
Which we are used to
Not Logic as we Think we understand Logic
It is not the Logic of School
It is not the Logic of Mathematics

It is a Logic
Which *Knows*
That Apparent Circumstances
External Forces
Are All *Irrelevant*
And always *Have* Been –
These are *Results* – Not *Cause*

It is a Logic
Which Knows
That the Only True Answer
To the Endless "Why?"s of Life
Really Is
BECAUSE

BE-CAUSE

It is a Logic
Which Knows
That Anything Is Possible
If we will
Consciously
BE-CAUSE

It is a Logic
Which Knows
That No Other Result Is Possible
When we
Consciously
BE-CAUSE

Responsibility – part 6

There is a certain kind of
Comfort
In This Knowing

We need no longer Wonder
"Why has this happened to Me?"
We need no longer Search Heaven and Earth
Ever Seeking
Someone
Something
Some Incredible Set of Circumstances
To *Blame*

Or Feel that we are Being Punished –
There is No Punishment
Because there is No Judgment

We need no longer Feel
Unworthy
Less Worthy –
All Are Equal

There is no Scale of Worthiness
Stretching from the Furthest Depths
To the Highest Heavens

There is Only Our Self

"I have created This"
Or "I have miss-created This"

If This is Not to my Liking
I Can Change This

————————

<u>Tranquil Balance</u>

The Mind
Is Not
Divided by Nature
It is a Single
System
With
Multiple-Focal-Points
Exchanging Thoughts
Feelings
Data
In All Directions
Multiple-Focal-Points
With no
One
More Important
More Valid than
Any Other
Our Seeming Parts
Created to Work
In Perfect Harmony
In Tranquil Balance
The Mind
Is not Divided
By Nature
It is the Ego only which Knows
A Sense of Separation
This Is the Job of the Ego
To Close
Its Eyes
Its Ears
To the Great Communion
Which Surrounds It
Which Embraces It
For the Ego, too
Is a Vital Part of this One System

<u>Law-Abiding Citizens</u>

"Ignorance of the Law" is
No Way to Live –
Especially after you *Learn* the Law
Then it goes from

Ignore-ance
To
Pure Stupidity

We Cannot *Not-Use* the Law!
It Is the Law of Life Itself!

So, Come On!
Let's All get Conscious

Let's All Be
Law-Abiding Citizens!

———————

Part two – on techniques

<u>Getting There</u>

I believe there are any number of Ways
And Combinations of Ways
Which allow us to sort of Get-a-Handle on
What and/or How
God IS

The Real *IS* –
Or at Least as close as our Human Minds can get
But no more Children's Stories
It's Time to Grow Up
We need to Understand that the Real God
IS
More Mysterious
More Awe Inspiring
And
More Unifying
Than any Children's Tales of "The Great Father"

I believe there are any number of Ways
And Combinations of Ways
Which allow us to sort of Get-a-Handle on
What and/or How
We *ARE*

The Real *ARE* –
Or at Least as close as our Human Minds can Imagine
We *ARE*
The Children of God, the Creator
It is Time to Grow Up
It is Time to Accept that
We *ARE* Creators!

It is Time to correct some Errors
To Create Anew
It is Time at last to Create the World
Which we have So Long Dreamt

There are any number of Ways –
But the How is not important
The Important Part is Getting There

<u>One Path</u>

There are Countless Paths
And No Two
Will ever walk the Exact Same Path –

Many may walk
Similar Paths
And Many Paths Cross
Become momentarily One
Diverge
Perhaps Cross Again

Yet We Each Have One Path

Though it may Twist and Turn
Upon Itself
Lead to Seeming Dead-Ends
Meander Aimlessly
for Miles and Days
Take Us to the Darkest Depths
And the Highest Mountains

Know Always – This Is Your Path

It is for No Other
To Walk
To Judge

We Each Have One Path
It Is the Path You Now Walk
It Is *Your* Path

———————

LITTLE STEPS

We need to Start
Somewhere
Somehow
Upon this Journey
And I *Know* – Every Great Journey starts
With the First Step…

But I think – Too Often
We try to cross **Worlds** in that One Step
We seek to Stand upon the Peak of the Mountain
Before we have Walked in the Valley

We Stretch these New Legs
Too Far
And upon Falling Short
Or Falling Altogether
We Cry Out in our Pain
"This Does Not Work!"
And we Turn Away –

We need to Start with Little Steps

CHOOSE to Feel Happiness
For Five Minutes!
If we Only make it For 45 seconds – That's OK!
It's a Start!
If next time it's Only 30 seconds – That's OK!
Just keep taking
LITTLE STEPS

Every Journey IS Different
But Each of our Roads
Will lead to Joy
Each of our Journeys
Will end in Peace

How Many Steps we Walk
Or How Long our Stride
Makes No Difference

Little Steps
Will still complete the Journey

———————

<u>The Twelve Step Approach</u>

4. BELIEVE
   3. TELL yourself the Truth
      2. TALK to yourself
         1. LISTEN to yourself

      8. BELIEVE
         7. TELL Yourself The Truth
      6. TALK to Yourself
      5. LISTEN to Yourself

9. LISTEN To Your Self
10. TALK To Your Self
11. TELL The Truth Of Your Self
12. BELIEVE In Your Self

Nature Abhors A Vacuum

Nature Abhors a Vacuum
She will not Tolerate Emptiness

Even the Vastness of Intergalactic Space
Once thought to be Empty
Is Now Known to be Filled Beyond our Imagining

Invisible to our Natural Senses
Science Now Declares
The Invisible
The Unseen
IS As Real As
All Which We See Before Us Now

And So It Is
With Our Own Minds
The Thoughts which Fill
Our Consciousness –
We can never Truly
Empty Our Minds –

We may Slow
The Never-Ending Train of Thoughts
To Examine
To Choose
To Reject

And We may Travel
Beyond our Thoughts
Behind Them –
But That Leads to a Fullness
Beyond Description
So it is that We
Are Never
Empty
So it is that We
May not simply Banish
The Unwanted

Nature Abhors a Vacuum

We are given No Alternative but
To Replace
The Unwanted With the Wanted
There Is No Other Formula
There Is No Other Process

Replacement Policy

(or Look! I got a New...)

We Live in a Disposable-World

It should NOT be a Great Stretch of the Imagination
To see Ourself
Throwing Away
Old Thoughts
and Old Beliefs

Replacing them with
Happier Thoughts
More Fulfilling Beliefs

Twenty-First Century Ideas

We are Here
To Evolve and
Help Others Evolve

To Help God Evolve

We Are Here to Enjoy Life!
We Are Here to
Express the Abundance of the Universe!

Just Think of this as an old style Life-Saving Class:

In with the New
Out with the Old
In with the New
Out with the Old

In With the New

———————————

"But, That's Lying to Yourself"

Well – Yes, it Does Feel like a Lie
At the Start
But even in that light
It's a Much Better Lie
Than the ones we're telling ourselves Now

And there are   Two Things to Keep in Mind –
First: If we repeat a Lie
Often Enough
Even *We* will start to Believe It

Second : The Truth
Is What We Believe
It Is

So, like the lady said:
"Talk to me, Honey – I Like it;
Lie to me, Baby – I'll Believe You"

––––––––––––––

"I have done that" says my memory.
"I cannot have done that" – *says my pride,*
and remains adamant.
At last – memory yields.
Nietzsche

Handicapped By Logic

We are *Not* Stupid!
The Complete Human
Is Genius in Action
But Very Few of Us Are Complete
We lack the *Balance* of Completeness

We Deny our Emotions
Forcing All of Life into Patterns
Friendly to – Familiar to –
The Rational Mind

And the Ego claims Undue Prominence –
The Ego is only Middle Management
The *Ego* is *the Straw-Boss* of our *Doings*

It is the *Heart* which is *our True Guide*
The True Director of our Life
The Miracle-Worker of the Universe

But We so often Keep our Hearts
Bound by the Chains of Limited Logic

To *Know*
Our *Thoughts* – Our *Beliefs*
Create the Experience of our Life
Just *Feels Wrong – Illogical*
We *Feel* the World as a *Great Mechanism*
Turning, Turning
Beyond our Control

And in *That* Believing
We have Handicapped our True Self
Bound the Power within Us
That None may See – Not even Ourself

We have been Too well Trained
In the Not-Trusting of our Own Heart
Too well Convinced that We are Not Worthy
We Believe that only our Logic can Make It Happen
That the Ego can Force it to Happen
That the Reasoning Mind can Conquer All

Logic Is a Great Aid to Understanding

I have followed My Logic
Through the Logic of a Twelve Year Old
Into the Logic of Quantum Physics

Logic can take us *Far* on Our Journey
But when We reach the End of Logic
It turns to *Handicap*
And Must be left to Its Place
While We Go Finally Within

Logic must be *Balanced* with *Feeling*
Balanced with *Intuitive Knowing*
Balanced with the *Wonder of Being*

I have learned there is Great Logic
In the Old Saying:
"If you Do Not Go Within –
You will Go Without"

———————

AFFIRMATIONS

Affirmations:
Cognitive Behavioral Modification –
SEEDS!

We Can Not
Have a Garden
By simply acquiring a Packet of Seeds
Throw the Packet in a drawer
Then walking one day in the backyard
Start picking up
Ripe Tomatoes

DUH!

We Will Not Wake Up
Tomorrow
And See *Avatars*
in the Mirror –

SEEDS!

———

Plant your Seeds in Faith –
Then Tend to the needs of Today

<u>Tending the Garden</u>

Water
Feed
Make it a Fertile
Environment

Have Faith!

This has been Proven
Shown
Time and Again
Time and Again

Time and Again – How can we Not
Believe
?

The Seed Knows

It KNOWS

!

IT
Will
Become!

Are We Less
than
A Seed?

Have Faith!
KNOW
BELIEVE

TEND
!
This New Garden

———

<u>Getting What We Want</u>

I guess I was like most people
Thinking
"Desire"
Was *"Wanting"*
But the Universe has
A Slightly Different Take on Desire

The Universe *Does* give us what we Most Desire!

But, the Universe
Being Intelligent
Assumes that what you *Most* Desire
Is That which you *Think About Most*
What you have the Greatest *Emotional Bond* With

This *IS* Logical –
Why would someone spend all
Their Time and Energy
Thinking about Something
They *Didn't Want*
?

Yet, So Often –
Instead of Focusing on our *Goals*
We put all our Energy
All our Attention into Imagining
All-the-Possible-Other-Things-That-Could-Happen

So, when the Universe Sees
And Feels
What we *"Most Desire"* –
BINGO!
We get what We *"Wanted"*

There was a Great Teacher who said,
"Ask and ye shall Receive"
There was no Sub-Clause
Specifying that *Worry* would *Guarantee Faster Delivery*

That Part is just Urban Legend

———————————————

<u>On Destroying the Ego</u>

There are So Many Systems
Which Declare that
The Ego
Must be Destroyed
Before we can truly Commune with our *Inner Being* –

In the words of the immortal, Sherman Potter,
"Horse-Hockey!"

We cannot *Live* without *Beliefs*
Without *Thoughts*
Without *Emotions*
They Blend into the Air We Breathe
They Are Part of Our Bodies
Our Muscles and Organs

Nor can We *Live* without an *Ego*
It is the *Soul's Most-Physical Face*
It is *That which Interacts with This Reality*
It Too is Part Of
Who We Are
What We Are

I Believe that even our Greater Self
The Totality of Our Self
Has Some Part of *ItSelf* which is Analogous to the *Ego*
For No Matter How Far Removed
From Physical Reality –
I Am
Still
ME

*"As it is Above,
So Below"*

———————

*To Deny or Destroy
a Portion of the Self
In an Effort
To Discover the Totality of the Self –*

Well, 'nough said...

Honest To God

This Lesson too has been Taught
And Taught Again –
To Thine Own Self be True

And We think We Understand –
Follow your Heart
Be True to your Own Values
Yadda – Yadda!

But there's More *To* It
And maybe because it lacks in
Glamour and Outward Showiness
We tend to overlook it

To *Ourselves* We Need to Be
Honest
With Ourselves
We Need to
Speak Truth
Not Lies

It is the Little Lies –
Tomorrow I'll cut the grass
Tomorrow I'll clean out the garage
Tomorrow I'll Start
Exercising
Meditating

And on the Morrow We
Remember
But We do not *Do*

And our Inner Self
Responds as a Child
Hurt and Not Understanding
Why We have Lied?

And again like Child
Our Inner Self forgives Us
And Again
Believes Us

But Again We Lie to our Self
And Again and Again
Until the Inner Self
Will No Longer Believe

And no matter How Fervent
Our Cries
No matter How Sincere
We Sound
The Inner Self
Will Turn Away

For It Knows We Are Liars
Our Words Cannot Be Trusted

It is the Little Lies –
Saying We Feel Fine
When We *Feel* Terrible
Saying Everything is Fine
When Everything is *Not* Fine

Our Inner Self Does Not Understand –
Is This How We *Want* to Feel?
Is This How We *Want* Our Life To Be?

When we Lie to Our Self
The Universe No Longer *Knows*
What to *Believe*
What to *Do*

To Thine Own Self be True

We Must Be
Honest to God

———————

<u>WATCHYOMOUTH!</u>

Watchyomouth!

This Really *IS* Step One
THEE Beginning Point
The Base from Which
We may Start Our Journeys
Our Excursions
Into Our Own Consciousness

Watch-Your-Mouth!

Listen!
To the Words *You* Speak
The Thoughts they Convey – the Emotions
The Beliefs

If we *Speak **of** Evil*
It *IS*
An *Invitation **to** Evil*

If we Speak in Judgment
We Hinder the Other
Hinder The Universe Itself
We Interfere with the Flow of Life
(Our Own Included)

We Speak without Forethought
Without true Consideration
And Too Freely We give *Emotion* to our Words
Adding to Their Power!

Our *Words*
Powered by Emotion and Belief
Are Given unto the Universe
Scattering across the Heavens
And Ever Returning Unto Us
In *Like Form*

We must Learn
Better Words
Better Thoughts
Better Emotions

For *These*
Are Gifts
Unto Our Own Self

ReThinking Words

Perhaps an Entirely New
Language
Is not really necessary –

Perhaps
We need only
ReThink
The *Words* we Use –
Remember the Original Meanings
Consider
Alternate Meanings

"Sin" originally meant
"To miss the Center of the Target"
(To Miss the Main-Point)
It had NOTHING to do with
Judgment by God
(Only Poor *Understanding* by Man)

"Nowhere" can also be *"Now Here"*

"Responsibility" –
Is this Duty
Or Guilt?
Or the *Ability* to *Respond*
As we Choose
?

We Too Often Use Words
Without Really
Thinking About the Full-Meanings
The Full-Potential of the Word

We say "I Need" –
Does this mean
An Actual Requirement?
Or, are we saying
"I *Want*"?

Words Are
the *Physical Expression* of
Our *Thoughts* and *Emotions*
The *Expression* of
That which We Are *Attracting*
Into Our Life

Is it not Better
To Experience *At-One-Ment*
Than
Needlessly Seek
Atonement
?

Perhaps
We Need to
ReThink
The *Words* We Use
ReFeel
The *Emotions*
Beneath the
Words

———

<u>Want vs Desire</u>

Finally We Learn
Finally We Accept
That
We Create Our Own Reality

Finally We Recognize
That Our Thoughts
Our Emotions
Are *The Building Blocks* of Our World

But Again We start to Fear

We Fear Our Emotions –
But Accepted, in 90 seconds
Our Emotions will have Run Their Course
Through the Body
And We may Choose New Emotions
Thereby Healing Ourself from the Unwanted

And We Fear Our Thoughts –
But Our Thoughts may be More Quickly
Turned to the Wanted Thought
Or at least Turned From The Unwanted
Thereby Nullifying the Power of *that* Thought

Now We are Told
Certain Words
Hold Negative Connotations
And that We should Avoid
This Word or That Word

152

But Like the Gun which Kills –
This Word or That Word Has No Intent
It is the *Intent Behind* the Gun
It is the *Feeling Beneath* the Word
Which May Bring Harm

Do We *Want* with Joy
With True Anticipation?
Do We *Desire*
From a Sense of Lack
A Belief in Limitation?

To Fear a Word
Or
Fear a Thought
Or Emotion
Is
To Miss the Point

We Are Free
We are Free to Choose
We are Free to Change

But What Must Be Changed
Is *Our Belief*
About the World
We Must Change the Way
We *Feel* About
Our Thoughts
Our Emotions
Our Words

We Must Learn To *Feel* What We Want
To Feel
That *What* We Desire
Is Already
Here Now
In Limitless Supply

The Universe does not *Hear* Us –
It *Feels* Us
It *Feels* How We *Think*
It *Feels* How We *Believe*
It *Feels*
Our Motivation
Our Intent

Words are Only Symbols-For

<u>The Good-Eye</u>

Everyone has heard of *The Evil-Eye*
Many Fear its Power
Some wear Charms of Protection
Some cast Spells
"Avert!"

But the Evil-Eye *Cannot Be*
Defeated
Anymore than Evil Itself
Can be
Defeated
We must Learn
We can Never Win A Fight!

*To Win Any Fight
Is The Only Impossible Thing in the Universe*

Yet – Unwanted Things
Events
Experiences
May be Removed *Without* Fight
May be Sent Away
Without Contest
Without Struggle –

I Introduce to All *The Good-Eye*

The Good-Eye
Is virtually Unknown
Yet it Is
The Most Powerful Force in the Universe

The Good-Eye is The Ultimate Armor
Beyond Any man-made Forge
Beyond the Legendary Star-Steels of Ancient Heroes
Bringing Inconceivable Safety and Peace

The Good-Eye is
The Key to Freedom
To Life Unthreatened
To Life Unguarded

"Now!" you cry – *"I Must Have This Unstoppable Amulet
This Ultimate Talisman!"*

And You Do Not Understand –
This Ultimate *"Talisman"*
Cannot Be Purchased
At *Any* Price
You Already Possess The Good-Eye

It Is
Has Been
And Will Always Be
YOURS

The Good-Eye is No More Than This –
Choice and Focus

If We will Choose to *See* That Which We Call Good
To Focus Only Upon that which We see as Good
Upon that Which We Want
If We will *Imagine* the *Having* of These
The *Feeling* of These

And We Hold Focus
Unwavering
Then and Only Then
Will Evil and the Evil of Lack
Leave Our Knowing

This is the Power of The Good-Eye

Only through This Power
Only in This Way
May We Remove
The Unwanted from Our Life
Only when We
Cease Our *Attention*
Will the Unwanted
Fade from Our Experience
If
We will Use
The Good-Eye

———————

If you Like it –
Tell Everybody about it!

If you Don't Like it –
Don't Tell Anybody!

Do You Believe?

Do you *Believe?*

Brothers and Sisters!
Do You BELIEVE?

Do you Truly *Believe*
That What you Desire is Out There?

Do you Truly *Believe*
That *You* are *Worthy* of This?
Deserving of This?

Do you Truly *Believe*
That it is *Actually Possible* to
Have This
Do This
Be This
?

Do you Truly *Expect* This to Happen?

If you Truly Wish This to Become Real –
Every Answer Must Be an
Unqualified, Unhesitant
YES!

THIS Is the Faith of the Mustard Seed –

I Know that what I Desire Is Here
In Limitless Abundance
I Know that I Am Worthy of This –
I Am a Beloved Child of God

I Know that This Is Possible
That This Is Inevitable

This Is The Law!

Profound Universal Truth #5

You Cannot
Serve
Two Masters

BELIEVE

Believe you are Worthy

God is within You
You are within God
If God's not Worthy –
Who the Hell *is*?

Believe you are Deserving

God is within You
You are within God
If God's not Deserving –
Who the Hell *is*?

Know This Is Possible

God is within You
You are within God

All things are Possible with God

Believe!

Profound Universal Truth #10

The Universe
CONSPIRES
In Your Favor

<u>The Universe Will Provide</u>

It is So Easy
To *Know*
To have *No Doubt*
That
In the midst of This Crisis
This Calamity
That The Universe
Will
Provide For us

We've Seen it So Often –
Facing Disaster
Devastation
Loss
When Suddenly
New Opportunity is Presented
New Doors Opened
New Ways Found

We Trust this Will Happen

So Why do we *Doubt*
That the Little Things
The Every-Day-Living Kinds of Things
Will also be Provided
?

The Universe does not Recognize Size

It makes No Difference
Large or
Small
The Universe Will
Always
Provide For All

———————

Wanting Is Not *Enough*

Is it *Possible*
That we have
Learned
The *Wrong Way*
To *Want*
?

Is it Possible
That *Wanting*
has become
a Thing Unto Itself
A Great Circle of Energy
Holding
Desire
But Not *Fulfillment*
?

Is it
Possible
That
Wanting
Is Not Enough
?

We must Know by Now
That We Need
Focus upon our Desires
To Bring Them
Into Our Life

But If We Focus
Upon *the Wanting*
We Are Wrong –
For This Will Bring
Only More Wanting

To Focus upon Our Desire
Is To Fill Ourself With
The End-Result
As If It Were
Our Lover

To Think Always
About That Result
That Union Of
Desire and Reality
In the Eternal Now

To *See* It
To *Taste* It
To *Smell* It
To *Feel that Result*
Now

To *Feel That Result*
With Every Fiber of Our Being
We must *Know*
It Is *Already Ours*
Before
It Will *Be*

We must Want With Gratitude
We must Accept
Without Fear

————————

The Ultimate Question

How will I *Feel*
When This Desire Is Manifest
?

This is not meant to be a Trick Question –
It's a question which should be taken
Absolutely Literally

We *Know* Intellectually –
I will Feel
Good
Happy
Ecstatic

We can Each make Longer Lists
with Little Effort –
I will Feel
Relieved
Grateful

But such Lists show Only
What
We will Feel
They do not tell Us
How
We will *Feel*

To make a Change in our Life We must *Feel that Change Now*
To say:
"I am Happy"
Has no Power to Change
To say:
"I Will be Happy When..."
Is even Worse –
For then We are pushing
This *Change*
This Manifestation
Into some Nebulous and Non-Existent Future

To Say has No Power

We must *Feel* This
And
We must Feel This Now

What *Feelings* are *Like*

Music
Is what Feelings
*Sound Like**

Sculptures & Paintings
Are what Feelings
Look Like

Dance
Is how Feelings
Move

---

*inscription seen on a pendent necklace

Affirmations – part 2

Affirmations
are
The Truths We have Forgotten

Truths
We have Hidden behind Daily Cares

Truths
We have Buried beneath the Worries of Tomorrow

We Must Remember
Always
We Are Each The Master Of
Our Own Life

Affirmations
are
The Truths We have Forgotten

Affirmations
are
The Truths We Must Remember

Affirmations
are
The Seeds of Our Freedom

<u>Be Prepared</u>

I have a very dear friend who Believes
We should Consider All the Possibilities
"Just to be Prepared"

Once I would have Agreed
Readily and Completely
Not So Much Now…

The Problem is that we are
Broadcasting
Every moment of our Life

And Emotions are
The Most Powerful Broadcasters
The Most Powerful
Magnets of our Life Experience
And So many of the Negative, Unwanted Possibilities
Have Such *Strong Emotional Power*
If we Really Consider Them
It's Very Hard Not to Have
A Strong Emotional Reaction

Emotions are the Rocket-Fuel
Of Our
Thought-Becomes

And the *Stronger* the *Emotion*
The *Faster* they *Become*

And it does not matter if we Want it or Not –
The *Emotions* were Fired-Up
The Rocket's Burning
And Locked on Target – *Us!*

I think we need to Reconsider
Considering –

Stop Thinking 'Bout Shit
YOU
DON'T
WANT
!

I think most Everybody has a Pretty Good Idea
Of AllKindsofThingsThatCOULDHappen –
So let's Just Think About
WHAT WE WANT TO HAPPEN

Choose
What you Want –
Focus On
What you Want –

Get All-Excited about It
And
Be Prepared –

To Receive!

———————

Profound Universal Truth #93

As Ye Believe
So Shall Ye Speak
And So Shall Ye Have

———————

Profound Universal Truth #3

In Freedom you were Created
And In Freedom meant to Live

———————

Even Before

"Even Before Ye Ask –
It Has been Given unto Thee"

And now Science says this Also
　Is Truth
　　All Exists – Here and Now
　　　Awaiting Our Choices
　　　　That each may Manifest in Our Life

　　　　We are but the blink of an eye
　　　　　Away from our Greatest Desires
　　　　We need Only
　　　　　Know This
　　　　　　Feel This
　　　　　Accept This Truth

　　　　It Is as Close as Our Breath
　　　　It Is Already Here Now
　　　　Within Us
　　　　And Without Us
　　Now

If We can Truly Understand –
　If We can *Feel This Presence*
　　It Will Manifest *Without Hesitation* before Our Eyes
　　Right Now
　　　Right Here
　　　　As Solid and As Real
　　　　As the Earth Itself

　　　Everything We Desire Now
　　　And Everything We Will Ever Desire
　　Is Here Now
　Ours for the Asking
Ours for the *Allowing*

We Need Only Choose
　And Accept
　　But We must *Know* that it *Is*
　　　Here Now
　　　　We must *Believe* that it *Is* Ours

Now!

———————

All that Is, All that has ever Been,
and All that ever Will Be
Exists Now **Buddha**

<u>Getting There – part 2</u>

We cannot Think
That We will Awaken
One Morning to Realize that
At Last
We have Arrived!

Getting There is a Journey
Without End
A Going-to Destinations which *Are*
Eternal Surprises
Unimagined Wonders
Which are Rarely *Where*
We had Intended
So Many Steps Ago

We must Never Believe that
This
Is the End-Point
As If there could not be *Better-Still*

This Journey *Is* the *Getting There*

We must Remember Always
This Journey
Has
No Limits
No Boundaries
No Final-Destination

It Is *Eternal-Discovery*

It is *Getting There*
Not *Being There*

————————

FOLLOW

We are advised to Follow Our Bliss
Follow Our Joy

I'll get right on that –
Right after I'm back from shopping
And the lawn is mowed
And dinner is made
And the dishes are washed
and put away...

This-One just took me *Forever* to Understand –
We cannot Chase our Joy
As if it were something *outside* OurSelf
To be Caught and Held

Our Joy – Our Bliss
Is Here Now
As it has Always Been
Within our own Heart

It is Waiting Within
For Each of us to Allow It –
An Eternal Bud
Ready to Burst into Full Bloom

We cannot Seek elsewhere
Hoping to find it At Last

Feel It!

If we Allow this Blooming –
There is No Seeking
There is No Following

Our Own Joy will Carry Us
As it Flows Ever Outward Through our *Being*
Our Joy and Bliss will Buoy Us Up
In Every Action

Our Every Task will be
Transformed
Into a Prayer of Thanksgiving
A Song of Happiness
A Dance of Joy

We Must Allow Our Bliss
Allow Our Joy

────────────

The Pursuit of Happiness

We need return to an Older Definition
of the word
"Pursue"
Not the modern "Chasing"
But that known by our country's Founding Fathers:
"To Actively Engage in *Behavior* which
Leads To
The *Experience* of Happiness"

THIS is Not our *Right* – It is our *Duty to Self*
THIS Is Our Reason for *BEING*

To Live in Joy
To Experience
The Joy
Of just BEING

A Great Teacher said:
"Seek Ye First the Kingdom of Heaven,
And All
Shall be Added Unto You"

We must learn to *Pursue*
Our Happiness

We must remember
Our *Joy*
Is the Greatest Gift
Which We may Give unto the World

Good Attitude

*I Am
Good Enough!*

*I Am
Worthy!*

*I Am
Deserving!*

*I Am
God!*

*I Can Do
Whatever I Want
And
Nothing Can Stop Me
!*

*(And I don't even need a Good Reason
Don't need No Reason, 'Cept I Wanna –)*

So There!

———————

Part three – other considerations

<u>Nature Vs. Nurture</u>

Some Say
It Is Our Nature
Only –
Our Born
Mindset
Talents
And Tendencies

Others Declare
It Is Nurture Only –
That
There Is Nothing Beyond
What We are Given
As Children –

Are We Not Yet Ready
To See
That Both are Right
That Singly – or
Blending Together
Each *Has* Influence
?

Are We Not Yet Ready
To Understand
That Neither Matters
Now

That In the Infinite Present
We Are Free to *Be*
As We Choose
?

———————

<u>Profound Universal Truth #72</u>

You don't get to Where you are Going
By Worrying about where you've Been

———————

"What's Wrong With This Picture?"

Remember that Game?

What a Terrible Thing to Inflict upon our Children!
That is *Old Thinking*

The Truth is that
There Is Nothing *Wrong* With
This Picture!
It's just Different – It's Supposed to Be!

Even computer-controlled Machines
Cannot
Ever
Make Two Things which are Completely Identical

Same-Ness is Boring –
Do Not Bore the Universe – It Does Not Like It!

Same-Ness
Is Very Close to Being Dead

We come to This World
As Individuals
Each Totally Unique

And a World Awaits Us
Which *Wants* Same-Ness
But That World was Never Meant to Be
Our Home
That World is Only for Contrast
Blue & Orange
Green & Yellow
White & Black

We Each Come Here Empowered to Choose
Our *Own* Color
Empowered to Create
New Colors

We Come Here

To Dance In Rainbows!

And there *Is* Nothing *Wrong* With
This Picture

———————————————

Keep Thine Own Counsel

This is another Old Lesson which We don't Really Understand –
Keep Thine Own Counsel
aka: SHUT UP ABOUT IT!

Every Great Teacher since the Dawn of Time
Advises this course of action –
Or Non-Action, to be more precise
And
Just about Every System of Magic ever heard of Agrees

And here is the Reason, the Logic, the Science
Behind that Truth –
We Are All Connected

.

*Each person's Emotions and Beliefs
Effect Each and Every One of Us*

So – If you Tell someone else Your Heart's Desire
There is a very good chance that
Their Reaction will include
One or More of the following:

*Yeah, Right!
Dream On – It'll Never Happen!
Fat Chance!
Like **You** could Ever Do **That**...
What makes you think that **You Deserve** That?*
And the Ever Popular –
What Planet are you From?

It is Too Often Difficult to
Silence our *Own* Doubts –
We have no need for *Others*
To Doubt For Us

———

Thinking for Two

Pregnant women are encouraged
    To eat Healthy, Well Balanced, Regular meals
    They are reminded –
      "You're eating for Two now..."

We need to All *Consider* Ourselves as *Pregnant*

    Our Thoughts
    Are The Children of our Futures
    And All Children
    Belong to the Whole World

My Thoughts Will not bring Fortune *or* Mishap
    To Any Other
      But they are Like a potent Spice –
    They *Flavor* the Whole
      Each of Our Thoughts
        Adds Flavor to the World
      A subtle but Definite
        Influence

We need to Stop Thinking that We Are
    Separate
    Separated or
    Separable

We Are Not!

We are CONNECTED to
    Everything
    Everyone
    Always

    Our *Individuality* Is Unassailable!
    We Can Not Be Destroyed
    Or Lost In Any Way!
    We *Are* Eternal
    But we are *Not* Alone!

We need to Remember *We* are "thinking for two"
    Our Thoughts are Added unto the Universe
    Our Thoughts
    Are
      Gifts to the Whole World
      As Well as Our Self

———————

<u>The Spices of Life</u>

The Spices of Life –
Giving our Life *Flavor and Color*

Spices come in Two Basic Varieties –
Bitter and Sweet
And the Choice is Always Ours

Our Emotions
Are the only *True Spices of Life*
Depression or Happiness
Joy or Bitterness
Hate or Love
Compassion or Anger
The Emotions we *Choose*
Flavor All –

First the Heart and Mind
Then the Body
Then Outward into the World

They Seep into our Relationships
Into our Jobs
They spread throughout our Universe
Highlighting – Spotlighting – Events
Circumstances
Conditions
Which Add To *That* Emotion

Each Emotion will Draw To It
The *Experience-Of*
That Emotion

Our Emotions are Called Forth
In Response To our Thoughts
And Beliefs
Yet our *Emotions* Are
Ours For the Choosing
They Are Already Within Us

We may *Choose* to *Feel*
However we *Want*
Regardless the Circumstances
Regardless the Conditions
And *That Choosing*
Is our Ultimate Power

Life Is What We Make It –

Be Happy!

We often hear *"Be Happy"*
As if it were Our Choice
As if We had Something to Be Happy About

We Look around the World
At the Poverty
At the Lack
At the Abuse
At the Inhumanity
At the Wars and all their Pathetic Justifications

We see the Economic Disaster
The Iniquities
The Massive Lay-offs
The Closure of Century Old Businesses
It Appears the World is Coming to the
Sad and Rapid End
Of All that Has Been

The Solidity of the World is Crumbling
Before Our Eyes

What is there to Be Happy About?

And therein lies the Answer –
There is *Nothing* to Be Happy *About!*

We must Stop Looking around Us
For Reasons to Be Happy
For Things which will Make Us Happy
For People who will Make Us Happy

We must Realize Fully
That *Happiness*
Is Within Us Now

We must Realize Fully
That *Happiness* is a *Choice*

We must Learn
To *Be Happy*
Because
We *Want* to *Be Happy*

What We Want

What Do we *All* Want?
A Beautiful Home?
A New Car?
Lots of Money?

There are those who would Decry
These as Shallow-Wants
Selfishness in the Extreme
Un-Christian

But Our Schools
Our Society
Declare *These*
The Marks of Success
Badges of Honor
The Goals of Hard Work
These are our Just-Rewards

And These Declarations are All
Crap-on-a-Cracker!

"HAVING"
DENIES NO OTHER

·

It Is Human Nature
To Want the Best –
That is the *Inner Self* Recognizing
That We are Deserving of the Very Best

But *What* We All *Want*
Is *Not A Thing*
What We All *Want*
Is to *BE*
HAPPY

And although any *Thing*
May *Add-To our Happiness*
Houses and Cars and Money
Will Not *Give* Us Joy
Cannot *Bring* Happiness

Happiness is A Choice

We may Each
Choose to Be Happy Now
Happy Where We Are Now
Happy with What We Have Now

And If We will Celebrate *This*
Then *Better* will Follow
As Day after Dark

Our Own Happiness
Our Own Joy
Are the Greatest of Gifts
Which We may Share with the World

Choosing to Be Happy –
That is Devine-Selfishness at Its Very Best!

That Is for Each
What We *All* Want

CELEBRATE!

Celebrate The Victories
The Joys
of Others
As well as your Own

Celebrate
As If they *Were* your Own!

Celebrate All Victories
All Joys
As If they *Were* your Own!

This is The Message to send the Universe –
"I Love Winning"

If you Feel Jealous of Another's' Having –
You are Feeling
the Pain of Lack
the Emptiness of Wanting

"They" have denied you Nothing!
All is Available to Everyone – Always!

Believe
And
Celebrate All!

To Celebrate the Animal

We are not Like our Brethren
We are More Aware

But We Must Remember
"Lower Animal"
Does Not Mean
"Less Than" –
We Are All One
And We Are All Animals

We Human Animals
We Naked Apes
Would Do Well to Remember
Our *Animal-ness*
To Honor
Our Physicality

Run for No Other *Reason*
Than You Can!
Dance Naked under a Full Moon –
Feel the Air!
Feel *Your Animal-ness*
And *Remember*

We are *Not* Physical Creatures who
Sense the Spiritual

We Are Creatures of Spirit
Sensing This Physical Reality
We Are Spirit
Seeking Expression
Through
The Physicality of Our Bodies
Through
The Physicality of This Earth

And *This Spirit*
Celebrates
The *Animal* it *Is*

———————

<u>Dis-Allowing /Allowing</u>

We spend
So Much of Our Time
Dis-Allowing OurSelf –
Our Self

We Block Our Own *Divine-Spontaneity*
With
Worry
Guilt
Shame
Fear
Doubt

My God! (and I mean That Literally –)
It's only *Us*
It's
What *We Are!*

When God Created Man
He took a Big-Chunk each of
Robin Williams
and Bishop Fulton J. Sheen
Mother Teresa
and Whoopy Goldberg
Henry David Thoreau, Lenny Bruce
and the Son of Sam

All of This IS In All of Us

We Each Hold the Full Potential of the Universe Within

But there is Nothing to Fear
Nothing to Be Ashamed-Of –
As Mr. Dylan said,
"It's Alright, Ma – It's Life; and Life Only."

It Really Is Alright –
It Really Is All Right
Allowing Our Self to *BE*

<u>The One Commandment</u>

There is No heaven
No hell
There are no laws Graven is Stone
That must be Obeyed or Punished for the Breaking

But there Can Be
REAL SIN

We cannot Sin against God
God Does Not Judge
God Allows
And therein is Man's One Sin

We may Sin against our neighbors
And Greater Still
We may Sin against our Self

This One Sin
This *Only Sin* is:
To *Disallow*

To place One *Above* Another
To Choose *For* Another
To Deny Another's Choice
To place Any Limits upon Life
This Is Sin

There is only one *"Commandment"* –
Allow All to Be

_____

Don't be a No-It-All!

ALLOWING

Allowing
Is Freedom

Allowing
Is Freedom from Judgment

Not Freedom from Being Judged
But Freedom from The
Terrible-Burden of Judging the World
Judging All that Appears
As "Outside" Ourself
People
Events
Plants
Animals
Minerals
Metals
Bacteria
Ad Infinitum

It can easily reach a point of
Ad Nauseam

And far too often We Judge Ourself

We are Not Here to Judge!
Any One
Any Thing
Any Time

If we will *Accept* the Universe
As It Is
If we will *Allow* things
To Be

We Free
Both
The Universe
And OurSelf

Allowing The Truth

(for Sutton)

A friend tells me today
With Horror hiding quietly beneath her Words
Of Her First Encounter
With Stalwart-Fundamentalists
Those who Believe in The *Literal Word*

How they told her that *Dinosaurs*
Are Not Real –
They are only Elephant Bones
And the Bones of Whales and Crocodiles

*"It's all part of a Government Plot to Debunk Religion
They Are All In League with Satan"*

She does not yet Understand
That these people
Speak the Truth!
She does not yet Understand that
*THIS **IS** THEIR REALITY*

I Understand my friend's Utter Frustration
Utter Disbelief that Anyone Could
Ignore All the *Scientific Evidence*
But there is very little that can be Done
In the way of Showing t hem
Another Reality –
In the way of Changing their Minds

This is an Intelligent Woman
She is a Teacher
But she does not yet Understand
That It *Is* Alright
That It Is
All Right

That we were Never Meant
to See the World
The Way
Any Other Does

I am Learning At Last
To *Allow* the *Truth of Others*

———————————

<u>Give It Up!</u>

We need to just
STOP
Stop with all the Judgment-Shit!

We are So Conditioned to Judge
Do you Like this?
Or
Do you Dislike this?

It must be one or the other!

When are we gonna Learn
To Just Let It *BE*
?

We keep trying to Lock-up the Universe

We keep telling ourselves
THIS is the Way it Is
THIS
Is the ONLY Way!

When are we gonna Learn
?

There are More Ways
Than there are People

——————————————

Faith Is

Faith is Knowing
The Truth

Faith is Knowing
The Law

It is Not
A little "Belief" with three cups of "Hope" stirred in

Faith goes beyond Belief
Faith goes beyond Hope
Faith is *Knowing*

Faith is the same Absolute Conviction
Which says, I Am Alive
Right Here, Right Now

I Am Alive!

Faith, Hope, and Charity

Faith is KNOWING
Beyond any Question
Any Doubt –

Hope is the Optimistic-Pessimist
Nothing More
(But Better than Nothing)

Charity is ALLOWING
Allowing Others to Have Hope
Allowing Others to Have Faith

EVEN IF it is A Different Hope
A Different Faith
Than Your Own

The Watched Pot

"A watched pot never boils"
Or *So* it Seems

Time becomes deep sand dragging at feet
Sucking the energy from us –
We can Not see the Process
All that Appears is *Lack*

And That is What Draws us
That is what Focuses our Attention
That is what Fills our Consciousness

But, so long as there is Fire
No matter how Small
THE POT WILL BOIL!

This is the Law – There can Be no other Result

And So with Our Intent
So long as there is the Fire of our Desire
The Fire of Expectation
OUR INTENT MUST COME FORTH!

This is the Law – There can Be no other Result

It is Not Ours
To Watch the Pot
It is Ours
Only
To Choose the Recipe

———————————

If thou wouldst assume the Master's role
Wed unto Faith like a wife
Faith will sustain thee, nourish thy soul
And attain thee a mastery of life
U.S. Anderson
from *Three Magic Words*

Forgiveness

The Old Saw reads *Forgive and Forget*
To most of Us
It is Meaningless
Or Seemingly Impossible

There are Deeds which Seem
Impossible to Forgive
And these Seem even Harder To Forget

Yet to Not-Forgive Is
To *Hold-On-To*
To Ever Focus
Energy and Emotion
Upon That which *Is* No More

We Must Learn
That to Not-Forgive
Does Much More Harm to the Self
Than to any Other

To Not-Forgive Is
To Give Away Our *Own* Power
To Hold Our *Own* Self from Growth

We Learn to Forgive
When We Accept that
We Too
May have Committed
This Unforgivable Deed
That We *Each* hold Within
That *Possibility*

We Learn to Forgive
When We Let Go the Past

This is the Forgetting Part –
It is not some Magical Process
By Which We Can No Longer Recall
That Which Has Happened

It is a Choosing to *Live Now*
A Choosing to Give
Energy and Emotion to *This* Moment
And to the Future We Desire
To Accept that Only Now *Is*
Life

MOTIVATION

The same Act
The Exact same Any-Act
Can have one of only Two Primary Motivations
Love or *Fear*

Choosing to turn off a running faucet –
Does the hand reach out in Fear?
Seeing the Waters of the Earth
Polluted
Limited
Diminishing

Or does the hand reach out in Love?
Choosing only to Respect this Gift from Gaia
To Use This Much in Gratitude and Joy
Knowing there is Always Enough

Making Dinner – is this Just Another Chore?
A Drudgery that *Must* be Done
A Mechanical Process to do No More than
Keep the Body Alive

Or is This a Gift of Love?
The Pleasure of Making Something with Love
The Pleasure of Giving of the Self to Another
The Joy of This Act

And if we Act Only from Habit?
Without Any Consideration of Why
Because this is just the Way It Has Always Been
?

We need learn Always to Choose –
Choice is our Ultimate Source of Power
Our Ultimate Freedom

I Choose to Joyously Accept the Abundance of the World
With Gratitude and Love
I Choose to Act Always in Love
To Give Thought to All my Actions
To Act Always from *Choice*
To Grant All of my Acts *The Power of Choice*

To Choose Is
To Fully Live

FEAR

Fear is One of the Two Emotions

Love is the Running Towards Life
Fear is the Turning Away from Life

Fear is the Parent of
Hatred
Fear is the Parent of
Jealousy and
Envy
Fear is the Parent of
Failure
The Parent of *"I Can't!"*

Fear is the Great Pretender
Seemingly all powerful in its Tyrannical Reign
Yet Fear has Not One Iota of Power
But what We *Grant*

Fear is Only a *Tool* for our Use
A Compass to help Guide
It was *Never* designed to be Master

Yet *We* Have Granted unto *Fear*
Ultimate Power and Dominion over Our Self

We have even established for Fear
It's very own Army of Minions
That the Message of Fear may Spread over
The Entire World
– In Simulcast and Stereo –

The Airwaves are Filled with the Fear-Mongers
Looking Always for
The Worst in People
The Worst in Politics
The Worst in the Economy
The Worst in Weather
Always the Worst
The Most Terrifying Possibility

Always trying to Convince Us that We Are
Helpless – Hopeless
That We are Destined to Be
Victims –

Lies!   All Lies!

Fear Feeds the Very Things We Fear
Adding the Power of Emotion
To *Manifest*
The Very Things We Fear

But We are Not Powerless
Not Helpless

We were Given the Greatest Power of All
The *Ability to Choose*
The Ability to Create the Futures of
Our Choosing

We Have the Power to Banish Fear *Forever*
We Have the Choice to Accept the World with Love

We Have the Choice
To Focus upon What We Want –
To Act with Courage

And all the Children of Fear
Even unto Fear Itself
Will Wither in the
Absence of Our Attention

Without the Food of Our Thoughts
Fear Ceases to Be

———————————

Fear is the Mind-Killer.
Frank Herbert, *Dune*

<u>Pragmatic Approach</u>

Do you insist on Analyzing
The Wiring Schematics
Before you turn on the Headlights of your car?

Do you Research the Type and Location
Of your Local Power Station
Its Environmental Impact
Before you turn on the Light in your home?

Do you need to Study
Chemistry
Before you can take an aspirin?

Sometimes a little Pragmatism
Can go a Long Ways

Just Do It!

———————

<u>Profound Universal Truth #54</u>

You Can't Win –
            If you Don't Play

———————

Part four – bad behavior

<u>Hero Worship</u>

I guess there's not really any Big
　　Essential Difference
　　　　Between Someone
　　　　　　Crying out for Jesus to *"Save"* them
　　　　　　Or crying out *"Buddha, protect us"*
　　　　　　　Or the sorcerer casting a *Protection Spell*

　　　　　And Me, or some Other Seeker
　　　　Jumping on the latest
　　　Band-Wagon
　　Touting the Virtues of the Newest Guru
　The Newest System
Following Faithfully
Until We Declare This Too
　A Failure

I guess there's not really any Big
　　Essential Difference
　　　　Between Hero Worship
　　　　　And System Worship

　　　It still means
　　　Not a Single One of Us
　　Is
　Doing the Homework

The Avatars

They Each and Every One – *All*
Deserve our Gratitude
And Respect
But We give Them Much More –

We place Them Above Us
Declare Them as *Better-Than*
We *Idolize* Them
We *Worship* Them

What Incredible Bullshit!

Isn't Anybody *Listening*
?

Each and Every One of Them
Has Told Us
We Too have This Within
We are Each
Brothers and Sisters
Each Equal
To Them
!

"These things I have Done – Ye Shall Do – and Greater Still!"

We have been Created
Each of Us
To Be *Avatars*

And Greater Still!

————————

<u>Alone in an Ocean of Oneness</u>

Too Many of Us Feel
Completely Alone
One Small Soul
Against the Immensity of Life

And being Told of *The Great Oneness* Which *Is* Life
We *Fear* that *Sensing Of*
Our Undeniable Connectedness
We Fear This Ocean of All Encompassing Love

Some Fear that
That-Which-Is-Self
Will be Absorbed or Diluted into Virtual Non-Existence
They Fear *They* will be Lost Forever

I think More of Us
Are Afraid
We will be *"Found-Out"*
That in this *Ecstasy of Belonging*
We will be Suddenly
Snatched-Up by the Soul-Police
To be *Banished* – Driven Out to cries of, *Unclean!*
Unworthy!

But there are No Soul-Police – There is No Judgment

When We Travel Within
We Return but briefly
To the Home of our Birth

When We Touch *All-That-Is*
We Touch only our True Mother
And She Never Judges Her Children
She simply Embraces Us
And Being True Mother
Wraps Us in a Blanket of Love
And sends Us off again
To Be Eternally
OurSelf

We are Never Alone
In this Ocean of Oneness
And We can Never
Be Lost
In this Infinite Love

Here We may Lose only
Our Fear

———————

We Are

We Are All Prey of the *Black Magi*
The Dark Ones
Who take away Faith
Who steal Hope
Who crush Dreams

White Magic is for Growth
For Healing
For Expansion –
It Encourages
It Uplifts
It Celebrates
All

Black Magic is Fear –
Fear of the Other
Fear of the Real Self
Black Magic Stifles
It Suffocates
It Struggles Always to Control
Or Destroy

We Are All *Prey* of the *Black Magicians*

But *Who Are* these *Dark Magi*?
Who Are these who would crush the Soul?

We Are!

Each of Us who has ever *Once* Said
To Friend
To Child
To Lover
To Stranger
And Saddest of All
To *Ourself:*

"That will Never Work"
"That's just Dreaming"
"You're Wasting your Time"
"Face Reality"
"You're Stupid"
"You're Worthless"

Yes –
We Are the *Black Magi!*

———————————

Part five – afterthoughts

<u>Thought AND Emotion</u>

There are those who Say
Thought Controls All
And those who Say
Emotion is the Key to All

Yet Thought and Emotion Are Inseparable
Thought and Emotion
Are but Aspects of One Process

Thought Is
the Great Director
And Emotion Is
the Power which Creates

We Live in an Endless Sea of Thought
And Emotion is the Water of this Sea
Emotion is the Force of the Waves
The Depth of these Waters

Thoughts determine The Direction of the Waves
But it is the Water which Carves the Shore

<u>The Spiral of Life</u>

Our *Thoughts* Call Forth *Emotions In Kind*
Our Emotions attract Thoughts
Which Encourage More *Like Emotions*
To bring us More *Like Thoughts*
To call forth More *Like Emotions*
A Great Ever-Expanding Spiral
Carrying Us On

Thought Equals Emotion Equals Thought...

But We *Ever* Have the Power

To Change Our Own Great Spiral of Life
That Power Is Choice
Always Available
Always at Our Command

Ever may We Choose to Change

THE GUARANTEE

Thirty Days or Less!
– *Guaranteed* –

But please Note that No One is Including
The traditional "Money Back" portion

You pays yo' Money an' You takes yo' Chances

Chances are You Won't *DO* the Homework –
Physical Exercise is a Fine Example
Many Start – Few Finish

Studies Vary
But Most Agree it takes two or three Weeks
to Effectively Develop a New Habit

I lean toward three myself
So Three Weeks
To Develop a New Habit
One More to Really Confirm It

For Thirty Days and Thirty Nights
We Must Stay Focused
We Must *Know*
In Each Instant
That We Are God
That He, and She, and They Are All God

We Must *Live* In This Realm of *Knowing*
We Must Stay *LIVING* this Lesson
For Thirty Days and Thirty Nights
Each Moment
We Must Know Beyond All Doubt
Everything Is As It Should Be

We Must Remember
Each Moment
That What We *Experience Now*
Is What *We* Have *Created* In the *Past*
And As We Focus
Each Moment
Each Breath
In *The Now*
We Are *Creating*
Undeniable Future

If We Can Hold to This New Way
Without Waver
For Thirty Days and Thirty Nights
Then
And Only Then Will We Succeed – Guaranteed

<u>Going Against the Grain</u>

It's *Not* Easy to Do This!
To Stand Up Alone
In This Most Human Way
To Go Against the Grain

There Is Great Comfort In Mediocrity

There Is Familiarity
And Much Company
There Is the Comfort of
Accepting Responsibility
For Only a *Small* Portion of Our Life
Comfort in Blaming – Bad Luck
Bad Karma
Others –

It's *Not* Easy to Do This!
It Matters Not
That Many have Gone Before
That More Join Each Day
In This Great Seeking

There are Far More Who Still Look
Without
For Cause
For Blame
For Reason
Too Many Who Still Negate
The Power of the Spirit

There are Too Many
Who would Deny us Our Own Power
Simply Because
We Go Against *Their* Grain

It's *Not* Easy to Do This!
To Leave
Friends and Family
Behind
Oh, That We Could Carry With Us
Even One!

But Each Must Walk Their Path Alone

As None can Do This
For Us
We Can Not Do
For Any Other

It's *Not* Easy to Do This!
The Starting
The Staying Upon Our Path
The Going Against the Grain
Of Our *Own* Yesterdays

Going Against the Grain of
Our *Old "Truths"*

W.D.Y.S.T.T.N.S.?

Q. What Do You Say to The Nay-Sayers?
    A. _____

That
Is The Best Answer –
But if *Words* are needed, say only
That *This* is where
Your Life has Lead *You*

And assure them
They need not Agree with you
Nor are they Required
In any way to Emulate you

(Though your Soul Screams to Make them Understand!)

1. That's not your Soul – That's your Ego
2. You can Lead a horse to water...
3. Everything Is As It Should Be!

That pretty much covers it...

You may Invite them To
Investigate for Themselves...

<u>Love Enough</u>

We – Each of Us
      Do Have Enough Love
      We – Each of Us
          Must *Know* this Love Is Within Us *Now*
          We must Learn to *Feel* This Love
              That We may *Give Freely* of Its Essence

          We *Do* Each of Us Have
          Enough Love Within Us
      To Love
      Our Brothers and Our Sisters
      We Each of Us may Give This Great Love
Unto *All* who Share Our Life

    We may Each
   Give This Love
  As a Great Blessing
Unto the Whole World

We Have Enough Love for This
    We Do
      But We must Learn to Give this Love
      Firstly unto OurSelf
          For it is Only When We Love OurSelf
          That We *Do* Have Love Enough
             To Give unto Others

———————————

Chapter Five

Diet and Exercise

*"As a single footstep will not make a path on the earth,
so a single thought will not make a pathway in the mind.
To make a deep mental path, we must think over and over
the kind of thoughts we wish to dominate our lives."*
Henry David Thoreau

Part one – diets

The God Diet

Eat God
Drink God
Breathe God

Not like a Bible-Thumping
Qur'an-Pounding
Vedic-Screaming
Madman
!

Allow the *Idea of God*
To Rest Gently upon your Thoughts
It is All God

The Food we Eat
The Drink
The Very Air we Breath

It is All God
Manifesting in Infinite Variety

There is Nothing
But God
We are God

Allow the *Idea of God*
To Rest Gently upon your Thoughts
It is All God

Diet Food

South Beach
Adkins
Smith & Jones
Smith & Wesson
I Don't Care!

OK, I *do* kinda like the *Color Diet…*
But it's not the three servings of Red and two Blue part
I just think Food with lots of Colors
Looks Prettier!
I'm an Artist – I *Like* Pretty!

And I think it Tastes Better –
It kinda Sets the Mood
To Appreciate the Food
Before it's ever tasted

"But, what Food?!"

I've always Believed
Food Is Good
.

I Now Know
Eating with Gratitude
Eating with True Appreciation
With Joy
Will Do *More Good* for Your Body
Than all the diets and "health" foods you could ever eat

This is Especially True if you Feel
That you *Must* eat "This" to Be Healthy
That you *Must* avoid "That" to Be Healthy

I just don't Believe In
Good Food
Vs
Bad Food

If you are Hungry –
Food is Good!
If you are Thankful –
If you are Happy
Feeling Full
Food
Is Better!

<u>Profound Universal Truth #9</u>

Chocolate Helps!

————————

Part two – exercises

<u>Edible Exercise</u>

*"Push yourself to Notice
the Extraordinary
In the Ordinary"*
Dove® candy wrapper

I will *Look*
At EveryThing
At EveryOne
As If
I have Never Before
SEEN!

I will *Listen*
To these Words
To these Sounds
As If
I have Never Before
HEARD!

I will *Allow*
The Wonders of the Universe
To enter my Consciousness
Without Judgment
Without Even
The *Judgment of Memory*

*I will See Anew
I will Hear Anew*

*I will Allow the Universe
To Reveal Itself
In Its True Splendor*

———————————

<u>Affirm Yourself</u>

Always
All Ways
Affirm YourSelf

This does not mean
Twenty extra reps on the Bowflex®
This does not mean
"I'm Right; You're Wrong – Nah Nah!"

It means to
Look at Yourself
With Love
And with Respect

It means to *Look* at Yourself
And Know
There Really Is
More than Meets the Eye...

It means to Know
You Have the Right
To Be Here

You Belong Here

It means to *Remind* Yourself
Always
All Ways
That You *Are*
A Beloved Child of Creation
That You Are Worthy

Your Self-Worth Is Beyond Measure

Affirm YourSelf
All Ways
Always

———

Childlike

Be as a Child again!

Children Do Not Doubt
They Know

When they play Make-Believe
They are Not Playing

They have Accepted
Without Doubt
Without Hesitation or Condition

THIS NEW REALITY

They have Created the World They Desire
And the Old World
Is No More
!

We need Learn
To Be
More Childlike

Exercise #28

Let's play Make-Believe!
Let's Pretend that
the World *is* a Good Place
Let's Pretend that
the World *is* Ruled by Love

Love for Each Other
Seeing Only the Best in Each

Love for All Creatures
Knowing
Each has a Special Purpose

Knowing
Each *Is* Unique
Even in their Oceans of *Sameness*

Love for our Mother Earth –
Gaia, I Love You!

Let's Pretend
This Is the Way the World Really Is!

(Play Make-Believe for at least Five Minutes Each Day)

Exercise #13

We need to Practice
Feeling
Our Feelings

First to *Sense* Them
Whether Blatant or Subtle
To Develop Our
Awareness
Of these Feelings which Color Our Life

We need to Exercise both
Memory and Imagination
To Capture
Not just a Name
But the *True Essence* of these Feelings

The Deep Tones
Of these Emotions

The *Subtlety* Of
This Feeling
versus
That Feeling

We must Practice Daily
That We may *Call Forth*
Any Feeling
Any Time
Any Place

Our Feelings are At Our Disposal
To Use
At Our Choosing

Our Feelings
Are Our Keys to Happiness
Our Feelings
Are Our Keys to the Universe

We need to Practice
Feeling
Our Feelings

———————

♪Forget Your Troubles – Come On Get Happy♪

Forget Everything!

Forget your House
Forget your Job
Forget your Car
Forget your Food
Forget your Family
Forget your Friends
Forget your Pets
Forget your Body
Forget your Name

Remember Only *This* –
You are Free!

Now – Get Happy About It!
Laugh Out Loud
Sing-Dance
Happy
!

This is the Most Absolutely Wonderful Thing
In all the Universe!
You Are Free

You are Safe
You are Unstoppable!
The Entire Cosmos Conspires for Your Benefit

Get Happy about it!

(Do This At Least Once a Week –
I think Once a Day is even Better)

———————————

<u>Workout</u>

We need to Start Exercising!
We need to have a
Daily Workout Plan –
Multiple Reps of *Self Love*
as We Brush our Teeth

Sets *of Positive Beliefs*
Lifted from Within
And Raised to the Heavens
as We Brush our Hair

We need to Breathe Deeply
Of All that is OurSelf
Exhaling *only Gratitude*
as We Eat our Breakfast

Each night as We Ready ourselves for Sleep
We need Uplift
Our Emotions
Honoring Each –
for *They are the Children of Our Thoughts*

In Themselves Neither Good nor Bad –
Hatred
Desire
Fear
Love
Sorrow
Joy
They are *All* Part of What Makes Us – *Us*

(Isn't this more fun than crunches and push-ups?)

Emotions Are the Breath of the Soul

Exercise #3

SMILE!

Not an Artificial Shit-Eating Grin
Not an Unmoving Runway-Mask

Just Smile

Let your cheeks float-up a little
Let the corners of your mouth
Turn upwards a little

A Little Smile works Wonders

You don't even need to think of something that makes you Smile
Just Smile

And Focus on How it makes your Body
Feel
How it makes *You* Feel
Inside

Let that Small Smile
Uplift You

(Do This Once Each Hour)

<u>Two-For-One Exercise Plan</u>

There is an exercise for The Eyes
To Strengthen Them
By exercising their ability
To Focus on Different Objects/People/Etc
And to Quickly Change Focus –
Distance and Subject

It can be Performed
Walking
Sitting
Even Driving a car –

Pick an object that is fairly Distant
But something that is moving Toward you
Or something which you are moving Towards
Keep the object in Focus until it is almost in front of you
Then quickly change your focus to
Some other Distant object
And Repeat

(Do this exercise for Ten Minutes Once or Twice a Day)

With the Addition of a Single Thought
You can More than
Double the Benefit of this Exercise –

As you Focus upon the First Object
Tell yourself:
"This is God in Endless Manifestation"
"This is My *Self* in Endless Manifestation"
"All is One"

THIS
Is the Reality which Surrounds Us
We Are All Connected

And with Practice
We can Learn
To *See* this Other As Self
We can Learn to *Feel*
– however briefly –
This Other
As *Self*

———

Chapter Six

Prayers and Meditations

Jill Bolte Taylor wrote a truly beautiful and inspirational book, *My Stroke of Insight*, in which she gives this most concise and precise definition of Prayer: "... *whereby we use our mind to intentionally replace unwanted thought patterns with a chosen set of thought patterns...*"

Part one – prayers

Prayer of Change

I No Longer Fear Change

I Know Now that I am always Changing
Always Creating Anew
As I always Have

Change is The Way of All Life

I No Longer Fear Change

I Know Now that I Am
As I have Always Been

A Creature of Change

I No Longer See
What-Is
As any kind of Final Reality
For I am Creating a New and Better Reality
Right Now

I Choose to release my Old Ways of Thinking
I Choose to release the Negative Beliefs which I have held
I Now Consciously Choose the Changes in my Life

I Choose Now to Acknowledge
The Greater Reality of my Self

I Choose Now to Realize
This Power of Change

*I Choose Now
To Embrace Change*

———————

Prayer of Faith

I Create my Own Life

I do not *Struggle* to Do this
I do not have the Power to
Control the Universe

Yet I Know
The Universe Will
Bow to my Least Desire
For This is the Will of God

I need only Make Known my Desire
And the Entire Universe will work Through Me
To turn This Thought
Into Reality
For This is the Way of All Life

This is the Law of All Life

I do not Fear failure
Nor Struggle for success

If I Struggle to Force my will upon the World
I am only
Blocking the Power of the Universe
from
Flowing Through Me
Into Manifestation

I do not Strive
To Keep Faith

Faith is but Knowing

And I Know that All my Desires
Will be Fulfilled
For This is the Promise of God

I have only to Allow
And All Will Be Manifest

———

<u>Prayer of Worth</u>

I am a Devine Expression of the One Source
Created in the Image and Likeness
I have Limitless Potential

I am a Unique and Valuable Person

Just as *I* cannot see the World
Exactly As Any Other
No *Other* can see the World
Exactly
As I do

I am Worthy to Receive All I Desire

I Create the World I Desire
I Create My Own World

I am a Worthy and Deserving Person

The Great Truths which live within my Heart
Now Come Forth
In Joy and Love

I have No Boundaries but My Own Heart

I Create from my Heart
That I may Give unto the World

<u>Prayer of Love</u>

I AM
A Devine Manifestation of Love

I have been Created by the Great Mystery
Which Is Mother-Father of All

I AM
Created in Love
As I AM Lovingly Set Free

I AM
Pure Love Made Manifest in Flesh
That I may Better Know this World
For This World
Is
Flesh *AND* Spirit

This World is Great Mystery
BECOMING

Great Mystery is without Judgment

Therefore I shall Learn to Live
Without Judgment
I shall Learn to Live
In Love of All
None Higher, None Lower
For Great Mystery has Created All

I shall Learn to see All
Always with Eyes of Love
I shall Learn to see Myself
Always with Eyes of Love

I shall Learn to Lovingly Forgive the things of my Past
And Accept Myself
As I AM
Now

I AM
A Devine Manifestation of Love

———————

<u>Morning Prayer</u>

I Create Each of My Days
I Intend for Today
To Create a Good Day

I Intend for Today
To See Only what I Want to See
I Intend for Today
To Think Only what I Want to Think

I Know that I Create my *Experience of Life*
By *My Focus on Life*
Therefore *I Choose to Focus Only*
Upon That Which I Desire in My World

I Will Notice the Things I Desire in My Life –
Knowing that What I Want
Is Available

During This Day
I Will Notice *Only*
The Richness of Life
The Fullness of Life

I Will *Celebrate* the *Having's of Others*
The Winnings of Others

There Is More Than
Enough For All
And *None* are *Denied*
By *any Other's Choosing*

During This Day
I Will Think Only the Best of Others
I Will Understand Their Striving
And Wish Them Joy and Success

This Day I Will Fill My Mind with
Thoughts Of Abundance
Thoughts Of Health and Of Joy

There Is Within Me
All the Happiness of the Universe
All the Joy of Life
Is Within Me Now

I Turn Inward to This Happiness and Joy
And FEELING This
I Know the Universe Supports Me
In All I Choose

I Will Focus upon This Day
Through this Lens of Happiness and Joy
Basking in the Abundance of the Universe
The Fullness of My Own Life

I Create Each of My Days
And for This Day
I Intend to Create a Good Day

Evening Prayer

As I enter this Sleep Time –
I Allow my Mind and my Body to *Completely Relax*
I Allow my Mind and my Body to *Release*
All of the *Tensions* and All of the *Toxins* of this day

My Mind now returns to its Natural State of
Tranquil Balance
As My Body returns to its Natural State of
Good Health

As I enter this Sleep Time –
I Allow my Mind and my Body to Rejoin with
The *One Source*
To Drink Deeply of this Wine of Endless Love
And Know *All Is As It Should Be*
To Swim Freely through this Ocean of Healing Love
And Know *All Is Well*

As I enter this Sleep Time –
I will sing myself Softly to sleep With
Songs of Gratitude
And *Songs of Joy*
And *Songs of Faith*

All is Well
and
I Am Safe

<u>Prayer for Others</u>

God, Bless these Children
These Flowers
Of Thy Garden

Let Each
Prosper and Grow
In their Own Way

Great Mystery, Aid Each to Hear Thy Voice
Within their Heart

Let Each find their Own Path
Let Each find their Own
Highest Good

I see them Now
Each Shining in Their Glory
Each Healthy
And Joyful

And I give Thanks

———————

<u>Healing Prayer</u>

(for Stella)

I am *Willing* to Accept Health and Happiness back into my Life
I am *Ready* to Accept Health and Happiness back into my Life

I need not struggle or strain to do this
For I know that God has given me a Miraculous Body
That is capable of Great Healings

And I know that God will Add unto the Strength of my own Spirit
To Help my Body to Begin this Healing Journey

I need not struggle or strain to do this
I need only Believe
For the Strength of my Faith will make it so!

I know that God supports me
In my desire for Well-Being

Therefore I will no longer Fight against my Body

I Now Allow my Body
The Freedom to Heal Itself

My Body is Already Healing
Right Now

I will no longer Fight against my Body

I know that in the Past
I have been Angry with my Body
I have felt Frustrated
And even Betrayed by my Body

Now I Forgive these mistakes of my Past
Now I Accept All of Myself
As I Am – Right Now

Right Here – Right Now
Is the Start of my Healing Journey

Right Here – Right Now
I Have the Power to Heal my Body
And bring True Joy back into my Life

My Body is a Wonderful Creation of God
And that Great Spirit Lives within Me
Lives within my Body
I know Now – that if I Allow it
My Body will use the Strength of God Within
To Heal Itself

Therefore I not only Allow this Healing
I Choose this Healing
I Believe in this Healing

I know there is Wellness Within Me
Right Now
And I Allow this Wellness to Fill Me

I will no longer Fight against my Body

I Choose Now to Turn my Thoughts
Away from the pains and the ills of my Body
I Choose Now to Focus upon the *Well-Being* Within Me

My Good Health and True Happiness
Are Within Me Now

I Feel Them Stirring to Life
I Feel Them Growing Stronger
Right Now

I know Now that if I Hold my Focus
Upon this Dis-Ease
I Hold Back my Body's Natural Healing

Therefore I Choose Now to Focus my Attention
Upon the Feeling of Good Health

I know Now that if I use the Labels and Names Of any Dis-Ease
Or Claim it as my own by Stating:
"My Dis-Ease"
I again Hold Back my Body's Natural Healing

Therefore I Choose Now to Claim
My Health!

I will No Longer *Be* my Dis-Ease
I Choose Now to Be Myself

I need not struggle or strain to do this
I need Only Trust

I will still listen to the opinions of my physicians
I will still listen to their advice
But Now I will listen to their Words
As opinions
As advice

For Now I hear a Truer Voice
Within my Heart

It is the Voice of God inviting me Back to Good Health
Inviting me Back to a Vigorous and Active Life

And although I may still take, today
The doctor's advice and the doctor's medicines
I know Now that these are only minor aids – temporary help

I know Now that it is my Body Itself
Which Truly Does the Healing

I know Now that it is *God Within* which gives my Body
The Power to Heal Itself

I Choose Now to Trust the God Within

I Choose Now to Trust my Body
And to Listen to the Voice of my Body
I know Now that God loves my Body
And loves Me as I Am!

Therefore I will Respect this Love of God

I Choose *Now* to look upon my *Body*
With Love
I Choose *Now* to look upon my *Self*
With Love

As I Am Right Now

I Choose Now to Give Thanks
For this Miraculous Body
For this Miraculous Healing

For this Miraculous Life
Which has been Given unto Me!

I Choose Now to Believe

––––––––––––––

Profound Universal Truth #263

As you Heal your Self
You Heal the World

––––––––––––––

Prayer of Acceptance

Great Mystery
I Give Thanks!

I have Felt this Gift
Tasted its Sweetness in my Dreams
I Now Give Thanks
For
The *Reality* of *This* Manifestation

I Stand in Joy
For That which was Dream
Has Joined with Flesh
And I Am Filled with Thine Abundance

I Sing my Gratitude
To the Stars
My Joy Fills the Sky
My Happiness Fills the Oceans

Great Mystery
Look into my Heart
Behold my Thanks and Happiness
For They are Beyond Words

Great Mystery
I will Honor
This Gift

———————

<u>Prayer of Giving</u>

I will Greet Each I meet
With Love
Allowing the Great Love within my Heart
To Shine Brightly
To Flow Freely

I will Look for a Compliment
To Give
Or a Thank You Very Much

And if there are No Words
That I may Speak
I will Give to Each
A Silent Blessing
and
Prayers of Prospering

And each time that I Give Love onto Another
I shall remember to
Give Love onto MySelf
And Thank MySelf for Being

And I shall Remember
The Abundance which Surrounds Us
and
The Abundance which Fills Us

Part two – meditations

<u>HEALTH</u>

I think by now
We All Know
STRESS
Is Not Good for the Body

Worry, Anxiety
Fear
Create Bad Health
This is Medical, Scientific Fact

Is it That Much of a Stretch
To see that
FAITH and TRUST and LOVE
Can Create Good Health
?

<u>Think About This</u>

It is *Not* that God lives
Within Each of Us

Or even that God lives
Within *All* Things

The Thing to Remember is
that
WE
LIVE
WITHIN
GOD

There is *NOTHING* that is not God!

When we Realize this Fact
We will start to *See*
The God within All

When we *Feel* this Fact
We will be able to *Touch*
The God within All

God Sleeps in the Rock,
Dreams in the Plant,
Stirs in the Beast,
And Awakens in Man.
Sufi proverb

EARTHLING

I am Eagle, Hawk, Raven
Brown Pelican and Dragonfly

I am the Leaf
Riding the Wild Wind

I am the Sky

I am Dolphin, Shark, Manta Ray
Cuttlefish and River Otter

I am the Shell
Polished upon the Sand

I am the Waters of the Earth

I am Wolf, Elephant, Meerkat
Leopard and Alley Cat

I am Praying Mantis, Saltisid Spider, and Lady Bug
Butterfly and Bumble Bee

I am Orchid and Dandy Lion

I am Oak and Birch
Apple Tree, Pear, and Hawthorn

I am the Mountain
Watching All

I am Human
Man, Woman
American Indian, Chinese, Romani
Viking and Monk

I am Earthling

The Throne of Heaven

Call it the Inner Self
The Higher Self
The God-Within

It Is the very Deepest part of Our Totality

It is the very Point
Which Joins the All
To the Now and the Here
It is the Point
From which We can Look
In All Directions

It is the Point of Ultimate Power

It is the Throne of Heaven
Awaiting Us

———————

<u>Everything Is As It Should Be</u>

Everything Is As It Should Be

This does *Not* mean
It is the Way I *Want* it…
Nor does it mean
That it must *Stay*
This Way…

It means that I Recognize
That the Universe
Works Perfectly
It means that I Accept
Responsibility
For My Life

It means that I Realize
That My Life
My World
Have been Created and Ordered
According to the Beliefs I Hold
According to the Expectations
That Fill My Thoughts

Everything Is As It Should Be

This means that the Universe Works Perfectly
And I may Create Any World I Choose

Here and Now

———————

__Two Words of Power__

There are *Two Words*
Of Great Power

Each Word Alone
Manifests Great Power

Either Word
Spoken from Scream
to whisper

Even in
Their Sudden Appearance
as Thought

Will Call Forth
The *Strongest Emotion*
The *Strongest Reaction*

And *Rarely* is this *Reaction*
Pure
Simple

And Rarely is Only
One Emotion
Manifested

So Many Thoughts
So Many Emotions
Clamoring for Attention
Each Seeking the Forefront
As They cry out in Response

There are *Two Words*
Of Great Power

The First Word is
God

The Second Word is
Money

————

<u>God and Money</u>

It is Amazing
And somewhat Mysterious
Regarding the Reasons
Why
So many *Believe*

That *God* and *Money*
Are *Mutually Exclusive*

As If *Money*
Were any Different
Than *Air*

As If *God*
Were Not
the Essence of
All We Eat and Drink

———————————

<u>Profound Universal Truth #23</u>

Money
Cannot buy
Happiness –
But
It Can make a
Nice Down Payment!

———————————

GIFTS

Each Day
Is A Gift
And
Each Day Brings a Gift

Each Day we are
Presented with a Gift –
A Beauty
A Wonder
Even Something we may
Touch
Take with us

Something we may
Keep
Or Share
Or
Give to Another

Each Day
Is A Gift and
Each Day Brings a Gift

And the Very Best "Thank You"
We can Give
Is to Act upon the Desire of our Heart
To Give in Kind

To Share our Own Joy
To Offer a Gift to the World
A Blessing for that Beauty
A Prayer for Peace and Happiness
A simple Smile for all we Meet

232

Divine Inheritance

The Abundance of the Universe
Is Unending
Unstoppable by any but the self
And All are Entitled
All are Deserving

We Are All Beloved Children of the Universe

We are All
Heirs of the Divine –
Any and All is Ours for the Asking

Great Mystery
Denies None
And Our Having
Denies No Other

Unending Abundance
IS
The Divine Inheritance of All

The Way It All – Really Works

Desire
Imagine
Accept

.

That *Really*
IS
IT
!

Thanking the Flesh

I *Give Thanks*
    For My Body
      And I *Give Thanks*
      To My Body

        I *Thank My Cells*
          And My *Organs*
            For the *Good and Wonderful Jobs*
          They All Do

      I *Give Thanks*
      To The Flesh of My Body
     For Its *Amazing Ability to*
    Heal Itself

I *Give Thanks*
    To My Body
      For the *Pleasures* It Gives Me *Daily*
      For the Miracle of Movement

      I *Give Thanks*
        To The Flesh of My Body
          For the *Wonders* It Brings
      Through My Senses
       Sights
       Smells
      Sounds
     Tastes
    The Touch of Physical Reality

I *Give Reverence Unto*
    All My Body
      For I *Know that*
      The Totality of My Flesh
       Is the "Organ"
        Which *Literally Creates*
       My World

        No Truer Servant – No Greater Friend
        Than this Flesh

I Sing the Body Electric

Most people think of Electricity
As something that *flows* through the Wires
Like water through a Pipe

But the True Essence Of Electricity Is
Spontaneous Change

When We throw the Switch –
All is Electrified
Be it Inches or Miles
The Wire simply *Becomes* –
All At Once

It Assumes this New State
Completely
Without Hesitation

And We Each Live
Though
The Body Electric
Our Bodies Are Literally
Bioelectrical Transformers
They supply the Psycho-Emotional Electro-Magnetic
Energy
Which Forms Our World

Within Each of Us is the Power
To Be
The Power to
Assume
Any New State
Spontaneously

Let Us All Sing of the Body Electric!

Let Us Each
Turn On Our Own
Electricity

————

<u>*Arriving*</u>

Arriving is a *Process*
Not A Destination

It is a *State of Being*
Which is *Flowing*
Fluid
Ever Expanding
We *Arrive*
In Bits and Pieces
Big and Little
In Trickle and Torrent
Our World Growing
Inward *and* Outward
In Directions
Unmarked by Compass

All Roads Leading Within
And Ever Outward
At Once

Our *Joy* Is Our Only Measure
Our *Being* Is Our Only Clock

Arriving
Is the *Remembered-Learning*
That We Have Always
Been Here
Arriving
Is the *Sudden-Knowing*
That We *Will* Always
Be Here
Arriving Is Our Understanding
That *Getting There*
IS
The *Being Here of Life*

Growing
Changing
Evolving
Ever Constant
Ever New

Part three – affirmations

Affirmations – Cognitive Behavior Modifications – Use Them! Tape, Glue, Tack, and/or Nail them Every Where! Keep them Visible! Paint them on your Walls! Memorize Them! Use Them! A Thousand Times a Day! Have I mentioned that Affirmations Are Important?

I have yet to meet anyone who has not had a whole bunch of Negative Programming to overcome. Affirmations are one of the easiest and most effective ways of doing just That. Affirmations make good Handles for the Mind. They make Wonderful Doors to the Inner Self. Affirmations are Great Tools for the job – they don't weigh a lot, they're self adjusting to the task at hand, and they're Free!

Any Positive Statement may be the Affirmation which works for You. Use what Works for You! But if you want to Change Your Life you Must Change Your Thoughts About Your Life. There Is No Other Way.

I Am
A Devine Expression of Life
I Am Infinite
I Am Eternal
I Am

―――――

I Am
A Beloved Child of God
And
I Am Worthy of All my Desires

―――――

I Am a Unique and Valuable Person
And I Deserve All the Joy and Happiness of Life

―――――

The Universe
Conspires In My Favor

―――――

Everything Is As It Should Be

―――――

I Am Free

―――――

I Am God

―――――

Om Mani Padme Hum

―――――

Chapter Seven

Possibilities

"Whatever the Mind of Man can Conceive, It can Achieve."
W. Clement Stone

<u>Thoughtless Behavior</u>

WOW!

Just Absolutely
WOW!

I'm at work – just had a new customer
And when transaction is complete –
I become Aware of
A Great Wish
for Wellness

A Wondrous Sensation of
Love
Flowing
From
Me
Pouring Out
Into the World
!

I didn't even Think about it
It Just Happened –

Just Totally
WOW!

————

<u>Miracles</u>

I've always Believed
In Miracles
They always seemed like
A Natural Part of Life…

I've always felt that Miracles
– Big or Small –
Should be something that
Occur with Regularity!

Have You Had Your Miracle Today?

After nearly six decades
I'm Just Starting to Understand
Not the *How* – Just the Fact
We Are the Miracles

Our Life, Our Action
Our Existence
Everything
Is Miraculous!

Close your eyes –
You can Feel the Miracles!

———————————

<u>Could We All Just Try</u>

Could we all just Try
for One Day –

To Look upon the World
(and Ourselves)
Without Judgment

Could we all just Try
for One Day –

To Accept
The World the Way It Is
(Ourselves the Way We Are)

Could we all just Try
for One Day –

To Forget The Whole Concept of Right and Wrong
The Whole concept of Good and Bad
These are only Perspectives
Circumstances
Ever Changing

Could we all just Try
for One Day –

To Imagine a World
Without
Conflict
Without War
A World of Harmony

Could we all just Try
for One Day –

To Visualize People in
Joyful Togetherness
SHORT People   TALL People
People of Every *Shape*
Every Color   Every Nation
Holding Hands in a Great Dance

People wearing Turbans
People wearing Sombreros
Fedoras   Stetsons
Ball Caps   Scarves
Babushkas   Bowlers   and   People with Bare Heads

People wearing Every Type of Clothing
Shoes   Sandals
Boots and Bare Feet
Holding Hands in a Great Dance

An Endless Line of People
Swirling
Twisting past each other
So that *Each* Person
Sees each *Other* Person
Dancing   Dancing   Dancing

Until We Realize
We are All
Just People
We are All – *Just People Dancing!*

Could we all just Try
for One Day –

Can We?

Can We *Not-Believe*
? in ***Gravity***

Can We *Not-Believe*
? in ***Disease***

Can We *Not-Believe*
? in ***War***

Tens of Thousands of Years of History
Tens of Thousands of Wars
With Names Long Forgotten
Victims and Victors – All Dust

Can We *Not-Believe*
? in ***Death***

If We could even *Begin* to Fathom
The Depths of *Our Own Power* –
If We could Just *Begin*
To Truly *Believe*
In Our *Selves* –

Yes!
We Can!

The Re-Thunk Human

It is a Wondrous Thing –
This New-Human
This Human built upon New Thoughts
New Perspectives
Truer Paradigms

It is a Creature of
Fullness
A Creature of Joy

Its Eyes *See Anew*
A Thousand Worlds
All-At-Once!
Its *Mind* Understands
And Allows *the Heart*
To Guide
Allows
The Self to *Receive*

It is a Wondrous Thing –
This New-Human
It is a Creature of Flesh and Bone
Hunger and Desire
A Thing of Sensuality
And Sexuality

A Creature of True Spirituality
FEARLESS!

This New-Human
Looks Upon the World Before It
The Infinite Diversity
The Eternal Contrast
And Like the God of Genesis
Declares In Joy and Enthusiasm

It Is Good!

It is a Wondrous Thing –
This New-Human
It *Is* What
We Have Always Been
But *This New-Human*
Remembers!

This New-Human
Lives in *Unending Abundance*
This New-Human
Lives in *Unending Joy*
This New-Human
Lives in the *Promised Kingdom*
The House of Our Mother-Father
Heaven on Earth
This New-Human
Is the Start-of
The Age of the Avatars

That will be a Time when Children are
Taught First
That *They Are God*
And it will be a Time when
Each will be Allowed
To Discover Their Total Uniqueness

And a Time When Each
Will Be Encouraged To
Live Their Own Uniqueness

The World Will Work As One
Yet Each will Contribute
In Their Own Way

———————

December 21st, 2012

I. The End of the Mayan Calendar
The End of Time
Also the Start of the Next Cycle – the Fifth Sun –
(but too many ignore that little detail)

II. The End of the World As We Know It
(possibly...One might Hope!)

III. The Day of the Rapture
(that Too is possible –)

Maybe it's the *Exactness* of the Date –
But even *Smart* people just get *Stupid* about it
Even the people who view it with
Joyous Anticipation
Act like On *That* Date
At That Time
Something will *Happen To Us!*

Nothing can *Happen To Us! Ever!*
It just Doesn't Work That Way –
We Are What Happens *To Us*
Always and All Ways

And I'd take That Date as a Ballpark Figure
Give it a Week or Two
Maybe a couple of Months
Or We could even Create That Change *Now*

Nothing Is Preordained!

We Create Our Own World
Each and Every Day
Each and Every Moment
In the Infinite Reaches of Now
We Create the Now's to Come

And Each of Us Contributes
Each Adds Color
Flavor   Texture
To the Whole of the World

I Believe that in Some
Not So Distant Future
There Will come a Time of Great Change
A Time of
Many Awakening

I Believe that The
Time of Great Change
Is Happening
Right Now

The One-Millionth Rapture

The Rapture is Near at Hand
The Rapture is In Our Hands
But the Rapture will not come from On-High

It Will Open from Within
As the Most Delicate Sunrise
Whose First Rays Will
Illumine Our Total Being

It will Burst Forth from the Earth
As Spring-Blossoms
More Vibrant
More Alive
Than Any Bloom Before

The Rapture is Near –
As Close as our very Breath

Do Not Wait For It!
Embrace It Now
We *Can* Bring This into Our Heart
Into Our Life *Now*

And as Each Awakens
We Draw Closer the Day
All Will Awaken

The Day When All Will Be New

The Rapture is Near –
And like *the One-Hundredth Monkey*
We Are the Key

It does not even require a Majority
– Only Enough –
It's like some kind of Quantum-Fulcrum
Some Point after which Everything
Suddenly Shifts
And the Whole World Changes
And there *Will Be*
Heaven-on-Earth

But We – Each of Us – Are the Key
We must Unlock OurSelf Now

———————————

Reality Check

So – We Create Our Own World
We Really Do

We *Change* Our *Realities*
When We Change Our *Thinking*

But here's a Reality Check –
We cannot Change the World
By Willing it to Happen
We cannot
Right the Wrongs of the World –
Any Attempt to Do so
Is a Guarantee of Personal Disaster

But here's Another Reality Check –
We *can* Change the World
By Example

When We *Become*
The Way
We want the World to Be –
The World Will Notice
The Universe Will Notice

For We Will Each Shine in the Darkness of Our World

And the Universe Will Add to Our Light
And when *Enough Shine*
That Light will Reveal
The Good
And the Beauty
In All

The Universe Will Add to Our Light
And
All the World Will be New

---

kensho
(the little enlightenment)

Seeing
All
Sensing
All
Being
All
I Float
In a Space
Which is Outside of Space
I Am
In a Time
Which is Outside of Time
I Am a Single Focal Point
Touching Space
Touching Time
Touching All
I Am
Here and Now
Touching
The Infinite
I Am Everywhere
Here
And Now
I Am
Here and Now
Knowing
The Eternal
I Touch the Immensity
Of My Self
Knowing
I Am!

<u>WITHIN</u>

We Live Within God
As God Lives Within Us

Each to their Own Character
Each Experiencing
Each Being
Each Other

God gave us Each
Free Will
And God Serves Our Will
Freely
Gladly
Lovingly

And has for Each
A Unique and Special
Gift

If We will But
Go Within
And Give Thanks

———

"If you feel like you're too small to make a difference –
Then you've obviously never been in bed with a mosquito"
Michelle Walker

The Greatest Service

It is Said
By All the Great Teachers
By All the Wise
By All the Successful
"Be of Service"

To your Fellow Man
To your Community
To the World

But I think We All tend to Think
In Terms of "The Great Service"
Establishing a Charity
Or Service Organization
Or Perhaps making the Ten Million Dollar Contribution
Or Building a School or Hospital
Or Writing the Great American Novel
The Lists could Go On and On

But there is a Service Greater Still
Which requires No Money
And it requires No Time
For This Service can be Given
Only in the Now
And though it *Will* Benefit
The Future of All
It is Given Only
To the Now

It is At Once
The Simplest Thing
And the *Most Difficult Thing* of All

It is *This* –
To Look Anew
To See and Listen
Without Memory
Without Expectation

It is To See *Not* the Surface Only
Not What *Seems* to Be
But To See the *Great Potential*
The Undeniable *Worth*
Of *Each* and *Every*

To Recognize that
Circumstance and Situation
Are No More than
The Clothing of This Moment

To *Know* that *Each*
Is God
Being
To Know that *Each*
Is God
Becoming

To *See This*
Is
The Greatest Service

———————————

This Life

THIS
Is How Life was always *Meant*
To Be!
To greet Each Day
With Joy in Our Hearts
And Give Great Thanks
Unto the Universe!

To Each Day
Share Our Abundance
And Our Joy
With all We Meet

To Give Thanks
For This Miraculous Life
We have been Granted
Give Thanks
For this Wondrous Power
To Be!
This Power to Create Always
Through Unbounded Freedom
Through Absolute Abundance
Through Limitless Affluence

Our Joy will *Overflow* Us
Our Happiness
Will Know *No End*

This Life is
Truly Wondrous!
This Life is
Truly Heaven-on-Earth!

THIS
Is How Life was always *Meant*
To Be!

<u>Someday</u>

I Truly Believe that
Someday
We will be able to
View
The Things we Think of As
Stupid
Gross
Repulsive

Anything falling into
The General Category of:
*"Don't Want **That** in **My** Life!"*

And we will Smile
And Say
"Oh, that's just God,
Being Different"

I Know That Day Will Come

But I Truly Hope that
That
Someday
Is
Soon

———

INDEX OF POEMS BY TITLE

Printed in the United States
by Baker & Taylor Publisher Services